Acadia: The Complete Guide

Written & Photographed by James Kaiser
(except where otherwise noted)

Copy Editor: Carrie Petree
Editorial Assistant: Kelly Swartz
Photography Assistant: Joe Hanlon

Special thanks to everyone who provided comments and criticisms of early drafts of this book, including Wanda Moran and Ginny Reams at Acadia National Park, professors Bill Carpenter and Helen Hess at COA, and Rebecca Cole-Will at the Abbe Museum. Special thanks also goes out to Brooke Childrey and the entire staff at Acadia National Park, who are consistently friendly and wonderful.

As always, a *very* special thanks to my family and friends for keeping me partially sane and somewhat socially acceptable.

To order additional copies visit www.jameskaiser.com

Notice a Change?

Although all information in this guide has been exhaustively researched, names, phone numbers, and other details do change, and mistakes sometimes happen. If you encounter a change or mistake while using this guide, please send an email to **changes@jameskaiser.com**. Your input will help make future editions of this guide even better!

Author's note: All views and opinions expressed in this guide are solely my own. Some readers (many lacking a sense of humor) will undoubtedly take issue with my characterizations of certain island locations. My observations are based on years of living on and near Mount Desert Island, chatting and gossiping with locals and summer visitors of all dispositions and socioeconomic backgrounds—from fishermen to multimillionaires. I've done my best to portray the island's beauty *and* the island's warts for people eager to learn more about this fascinating place. What some readers will look down upon as crass gossip will undoubtedly be celebrated as "colorful history" in the decades to come. I'm just getting a head start.

Printed in Singapore

ACADIA

• THE COMPLETE GUIDE •

JAMES KAISER

don't

miss out

Top Attractions on Mount Desert Island

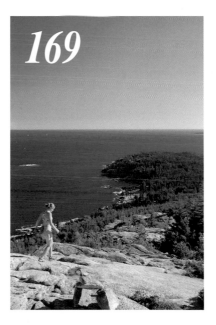

169 HIKING
130 miles of stunning trails that crisscross the island.

195 CARRIAGE ROADS
57 miles of exquisite roads, perfect for biking or horseback riding.

148 CADILLAC MOUNTAIN
360 degree views from the island's highest peak.

CONTENTS

Bar Harbor

CONGRATULATIONS!

I F YOU'VE PICKED up this book, you're going to Mount Desert Island. Perhaps you're already here. If so, you're in one of the most amazing places in the world—a gorgeous island filled with mountains that tumble to the sea, steeped in fascinating history and dripping with outdoor adventure. A place where you can hike in the morning, sea kayak in the afternoon, and sit down to a gourmet meal at night. If you're looking for five-star luxury surrounded by stunning natural beauty, look no further, my friends.

So who am I and why should you listen to me? My name is James Kaiser, and I'm the writer and photographer of this guide. I was born and raised near Mount Desert Island, spending my childhood summers hiking and biking in Acadia National Park and my college summers living and working in Bar Harbor. Although my work as a writer and photographer has carried me away from Mount Desert Island, I return as often as possible. It's my favorite place in the world. I know the park, I know the towns, I know the locals—I know the secrets! And I'm going to show you the best that the island has to offer.

You could easily spend a month on Mount Desert Island and not run out of things to do. But if you're like most people, you're only here for a few days. Make those few days count! With a limited amount of time, you've got to plan your trip wisely. This book will put the best of Mount Desert Island and Acadia National Park at your fingertips, helping you maximize your time for an unforgettable vacation. Whether you're here to hike, here to sightsee, or just here to eat and hang out, *Acadia: The Complete Guide* is the only guide you'll need.

Now let me show you the best that Mount Desert Island has to offer...

Champlain Mountain

Humpback Whale

Porcupine Islands

Carriage Road Bridge

SCHOODIC
PENINSULA

MOUNT
DESERT ISLAND

SWAN'S
ISLAND

ISLE AU
HAUT

ATLANTIC OCEAN

OVERVIEW

MOUNT DESERT ISLAND is the crown jewel of maritime New England. Located two-thirds of the way up the craggy coast of Maine, it's the only place on the East Coast where the mountains literally meet the sea. Those mountains, rounded and smoothed by Ice Age glaciers, form one of the most distinctive island profiles in the world. From sea they look like a string of giant ice cream scoops rising up out of the water. Cadillac Mountain, the island's tallest peak, is 1,532 feet—the highest point on the Atlantic north of Rio de Janeiro.

Nestled between the island's 24 mountain peaks are forests, lakes, meadows, marshes and the only fjord on the East Coast: Somes Sound, which nearly cuts the island in two. About a dozen coastal villages dot the shores of Mount Desert Island—some, like Bar Harbor, built around tourism, others, like Bass Harbor, carrying on as quiet fishing hamlets much as they always have. There are also wealthy summer communities like Seal Harbor and Northeast Harbor, and historic villages like Somesville, the island's oldest town. Several offshore islands such as the Cranberry Isles, Swan's Island, and Isle au Haut are accessible by ferry, making them great for day tripping.

Roughly two-thirds of Mount Desert Island has been set aside as Acadia National Park. At just 46,000 acres, Acadia is one of the smallest national parks in America. But it's also one of the most popular, luring roughly 3 million visitors a year. Acadia's most famous attraction is the Park Loop Road, which runs along the island's rugged eastern shore before cutting through the forest, passing by two pristine lakes, and twisting to the top of Cadillac Mountain. Acadia also boasts 130 miles of exquisite hiking trails and 57 miles of carriage roads for biking and horseback riding. In addition to land on Mount Desert Island, the park also includes Schoodic Peninsula (on the mainland) and half of Isle au Haut, a rugged island 14 miles southwest of Mount Desert Island.

In the days before Columbus, Mount Desert Island was the seasonal home of the Wabanaki Indians. Hardy coastal settlers arrived in the late 1700s, followed by artists and tourists several decades later. By the late 1800s, the island was one of the most exclusive summer resorts in America. But by the 1930s, the glamour of the island had started to fade. In 1947 a massive fire burned down many of the island's once-grand mansions, and following the fire the island rebuilt and reestablished itself as a major tourist mecca. Today it attracts a diverse mix of visitors: outdoor junkies, fanny-packed retirees, college students, hippies, and billionaires—proving there's something for everyone here.

Physically beautiful and culturally unique, Mount Desert Island is one of the most fascinating and fantastic islands in the world.

BASICS

GETTING TO MOUNT DESERT ISLAND

The good news is that you don't need a boat to get to Mount Desert Island (which is only an island by about 50 feet at low tide). A small bridge connects the island to the mainland. How you get to that bridge is up to you.

BY CAR

Driving your own car is the most popular way to get to Mount Desert Island. From southern Maine there are two options: the fast route and the scenic route. The fast route follows I-95 north to Bangor, heads east on I-395 to Route 1A, and follows Route 1A to Mount Desert Island (about a 3–4 hour drive from the Maine/New Hampshire border). The scenic route starts in Portland and follows Route 1 up the coast of Maine to Ellsworth. From there you'll connect with Route 1A to Mount Desert Island. Between Portland and Ellsworth, you'll pass through Rockland, Camden, and other gorgeous coastal towns. The scenic route takes about 5–6 hours from Portland (not counting weekend traffic).

BY PLANE

The **Hancock County/Bar Harbor Airport** (www.bhbairport.com) is located in the town of Trenton on the mainland, 12 miles from downtown Bar Harbor. In the summer, US Airways runs daily flights between Boston and Bar Harbor. The Island Explorer (p.19) runs free shuttles between the Bar Harbor Airport and downtown Bar Harbor from late June through August. Taxis and rental cars are also available year-round. The next closest airports are **Bangor International Airport** (located in Bangor, Maine, about a 1.5 hour drive from Mount Desert Island, www.flybangor.com) and **Portland International Jetport** (located in Portland, Maine, about a 3.5 hour drive from Mount Desert Island, www.portlandjetport.org).

BY BOAT

Although you don't *need* a boat to get to Mount Desert Island, that option is available. The high speed ferry *The Cat* runs daily trips between Bar Harbor and Yarmouth, Nova Scotia (www.thecat.com).

BY BUS

Vermont Transit offers daily bus service to Bar Harbor from Portland and Bangor (800-552-8737, www.vermonttransit.com).

GETTING AROUND MOUNT DESERT ISLAND

The best way to get around the island these days is the free Island Explorer Shuttle. These propane-powered buses were experimentally introduced in 1999 to reduce traffic and air pollution in the park. The experiment was wildly successful. Today, thanks to generous financial support from L.L. Bean, Friends of Acadia, and many local businesses, the Island Explorer runs seven routes linking hotels, inns, and campgrounds with popular destinations throughout the island. (An eighth bus route circles Schoodic Peninsula on the mainland.) Buses run from late June through mid-October, but service is scaled back after Labor Day. The hub of the system is the Bar Harbor Village Green, where all routes on the island begin or end (and where a giant, blinking map tracks the progress of each shuttle through GPS). Island Explorer maps and timetables are available at any visitor center and on the Island Explorer Web site, www.exploreacadia.com. The alternative to the Island Explorer is driving your own car, but parking can be a hassle at popular locations during the busy summer months. Unless you're going somewhere the Island Explorer doesn't go (the top of Cadillac Mountain, for example), it's often easier and more convenient to take the Island Explorer. If you don't have a car or the Island Explorer isn't running, Bar Harbor has two taxi companies: At Your Service Taxi (207-288-9222) and O-Pooch Taxi (207-288-3898).

VISITOR CENTERS

THOMPSON ISLAND VISITOR CENTER
Located on tiny Thompson Island, between Mount Desert Island and the mainland, this modest visitor center is a good place to ask questions and pick up free brochures and publications. The staff also keep track of lodging vacancies on the island. Open daily 10am–8pm, May to mid-October.

HULLS COVE VISITOR CENTER
Acadia National Park's main visitor center. See page 108.

ACADIA INFORMATION CENTER
A privately owned, advertiser-funded information center on Route 3 in Trenton (on the mainland). Offers free brochures, interactive displays, and a knowledgeable staff. (800-358-8550, www.acadiainfo.com).

CHAMBERS OF COMMERCE
Helpful for seasonal info and last-minute lodging.

Bar Harbor Chamber of Commerce (93 Cottage Street, Bar Harbor, 207-288-5103, www.barharborinfo.com).

Southwest Harbor/Tremont Chamber of Commerce (204 Main Street, Southwest Harbor, 207-244-9264, www.acadiachamber.com).

LODGING

There are dozens of places to stay on Mount Desert Island—hotels, motels, bed and breakfasts, ect.—and listing them here would take up dozens of pages. Rather than waste all that paper (when all you need is one room), I've posted all lodging information on www.jameskaiser.com. Suffice to say, the vast majority of lodging is found in Bar Harbor, though Northeast Harbor and Southwest Harbor also have some great lodging. No matter where you end up, however, the island is small enough that you'll never be too far from whatever it is you came here for. If you find room prices on the island prohibitively expensive, try looking in off-island towns such as Trenton or Ellsworth.

CAMPING

Acadia National Park runs two campgrounds on Mount Desert Island: Blackwoods and Seawall. Both are situated in the forest with no ocean views, and each has a maximum capacity of six people per site. There are also about a dozen private campgrounds located outside the park (posted at www.jameskaiser.com). In addition, Acadia operates Duck Harbor Campground on far-flung Isle au Haut (p.159).

BLACKWOODS

The most popular campground in Acadia. Blackwoods is located off Route 3 between Bar Harbor and Seal Harbor on the eastern side of Mount Desert Island, close to many of the island's top attractions. Reservations are required between June 15 and September 15. 300+ sites. Cost: $20 per night, April–November (800-365-2267, http://reservations.nps.gov).

SEAWALL

This first-come, first-served campground is located near the southwestern tip of Mount Desert Island. Some people love the remote location, others find it inconvenient. To snag a site in mid-summer arrive at 8:30am when the ranger station opens. Open Memorial Day Weekend through September. 200 sites. Cost: $20 per night.

WEATHER & WHEN TO GO

Let me introduce you to Maine's most tired and worn-out cliché: "If you don't like the weather, wait a minute. It'll change." But like all tired and worn-out clichés, it's tired and worn-out because it's true. The weather in Maine, especially along the coast, is psychotically unpredictable. It varies from day to day, month to month, and year to year. There's simply no rhyme or reason to it—as any local weatherman will attest (tough job, Maine weatherman). That being said, when the weather's good, it's incredible. And even when it's bad—foggy, rainy, snowy—the coast has its own beautiful mystique. Keep in mind that in terms of annual precipitation coastal Maine has been ranked second in America only to the Pacific Northwest. It can rain at any time of the year on short notice, so plan accordingly.

WEATHER & WHEN TO GO

SPRING

Otherwise known as Mud Season. Spring on Mount Desert Island definitely has its pros and cons. Melting snow and ice keep things soggy in the early spring, but by late spring the island has dried out and temperatures are often divine. Spring is also blackfly season, with the biting bugs most active between mid-May and mid-June when running water provides optimum breeding conditions. That being said, blackfly numbers depend considerably on how rainy it has been. Spring is also when local businesses come out of their long winter hibernation. Hotels and shops start opening in late April, and by Memorial Day the island is firing on all cylinders.

SUMMER

Sunny summer days bring perfect temperatures to Mount Desert Island: high 70s with a cool ocean breeze. But summer can also bring thick fogs that blanket the island for hours or sometimes days. Sunny or not, July is when things get busy on Mount Desert Island—booked hotels, waiting lists at restaurants, crowded parking lots, you name it. (This is all relative, of course. By Maine standards it's crazy, but New Yorkers will probably appreciate the peace and quiet.) August is even busier than July, and just when things seem like they can't get any crazier Labor Day hits and the season ends with a bang.

MOUNT DESERT ISLAND CLIMATE
(based on annual averages)

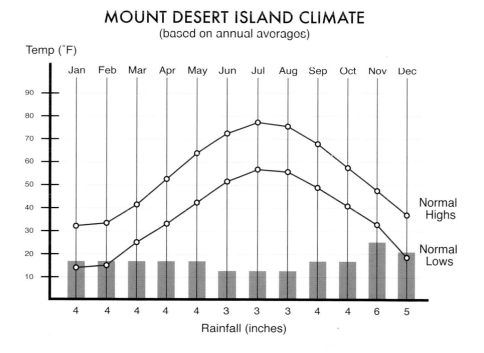

Coastal Maine Weather

WIND

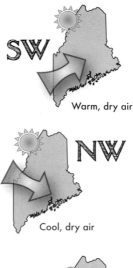

Warm, dry air

Cool, dry air

Cloudy, rainy

Nor'easter

Weather along the Maine coast is highly unpredictable. In fact, weather patterns here are more variable and more extreme than almost any other place in the United States. Conditions can change on a moment's notice, but you can still get a general sense of what lies ahead by reading the wind—just as sailors have done for hundreds of years. During the summer, prevailing winds blow from the southwest, bringing warm, dry air. Winds from the northwest bring cool, dry air, sweeping away moisture and creating spectacular visibility. Winds that blow from the east, however, are far less desirable. Southeasterly winds often bring overcast days with the possibility of fog and drizzle. And if the wind starts blowing from the northeast, a dreaded nor'easter could be on the way.

Nor'easters form when cold, arctic air blowing down from Canada collides with warm, tropical air moving up the East Coast. The collision creates a counterclockwise spinning cyclone, similar to a hurricane. As the cyclone moves offshore, winds blow from the northeast—hence the term "nor'easter." When they form offshore, nor'easters bring gale force winds, extreme surf, and massive amounts of rain. Remember *The Perfect Storm*? That was an offshore nor'easter. Onshore nor'easters are much less catastrophic; many are just regular storms. Although most common between October and April, nor'easters can form at any time of the year.

Finally there's hurricane season, which runs from June to November. Most hurricanes, however, dissipate on land long before reaching Maine. The rare hurricane that does hit generally arrives in August, September, or October.

"I reverently believe that the Maker who made us all makes everything in New England but the weather. I don't know who makes that, but I think it must be some raw apprentices in the weather-clerk's factory..."

—Mark Twain

Summer fog

WEATHER & WHEN TO GO

FALL

One of the best times to visit Mount Desert Island. The weather is crisp, the crowds are light, and the foliage is often spectacular. Weather in early September is often indistinguishable from late August, but temperatures always start dropping by the end of the month. The foliage usually peaks during the first two weeks of October, and it can sometimes linger for several weeks. By late October, however, temperatures start plummeting, tourists start departing en masse, and locals start hunkering down. By early November, many storefront windows in Bar Harbor are covered in plywood, and the island goes into hibernation for the winter.

WINTER

A cold, cold time to visit Mount Desert Island. New England has some of the longest and most ferocious winters of any region in the United States. And though the ocean warms things up a bit on the coast, that's not saying much. The average snowfall on Mount Desert Island is 60 inches, but the snow that falls often melts quickly. When the snow sticks, Acadia's carriage roads are great for cross country skiing. But most hotels, restaurants, museums, and other attractions are closed for the season, which make winter the least popular time to visit the island.

WHAT IS "DOWNEAST" MAINE?

Downeast Maine refers to the state's eastern coastal region. The term "Downeast" is derived from sailing terminology. The region's prevailing winds blow west, and ships departing from Boston or western Maine would sail *down*wind to travel *east*. Hence, Downeast.

CALENDAR

June	July	July
Legacy of the Arts **Bar Harbor** Summer arts show on the Village Green. Contact: Bar Harbor Chamber of Commerce.	**Fourth of July** **Bar Harbor** Pancake breakfast, outdoor concert, parade, fireworks. Contact: Bar Harbor Chamber of Commerce	**Native American Festival** **Bar Harbor** Native artists demonstrate traditional crafts including basket weaving. Contact: Abbe Museum.

September	October	October
Garlic Festival **Town Hill** Garlic and smoked foods festival. Contact: Atlantic Brewing Company.	**Octoberfest** **Southwest Harbor** Features beers from over 20 Maine microbreweries. Contact: Southwest Harbor Chamber of Commerce.	**MDI Marathon** **Mount Desert Island** Timed to coincide with fall foliage. Contact: Bar Harbor Chamber of Commerce.

WHAT TO BRING

When visiting Mount Desert Island, you can never be too prepared. Pack a swimsuit, pack a rain jacket, and pack everything else in between. Ignore whatever weather forecast you've heard (most are only good for a few hours, anyway) and pack clothes for hot weather, cold weather, and rainy weather. Don't worry if you forget something—there are plenty of shops in Bar Harbor (and a Wal-Mart in Ellsworth on the mainland).

ONE PERFECT DAY ON MOUNT DESERT ISLAND

Visiting Mount Desert Island for the first time? The following schedule serves up one perfect day on the island.

- Sunrise on Cadillac Mountain (p.148)
- Breakfast in Bar Harbor (p.221)
- Midmorning walk on the Bar Harbor Shore Path (p.213)
- Late-morning drive along the Park Loop Road (p.107)
- Lunch at the Jordan Pond House (p.138)
- Rent bikes in Bar Harbor and explore the carriage roads (p.195)
- Dinner at Thurston's Lobster Pound (p.251)
- Sunset at Bass Harbor Lighthouse (p.249)

*Other afternoon options: Whale Watching (p.217), Hike the Beehive (p.170)

ONE PERFECT DAY FOR THE OUTDOOR BUFF

If you're the type of person who loves to wake up at dawn and work your body to exhaustion, you'll *love* Mount Desert Island.

- 5am breakfast at Jordan's Restaurant in Bar Harbor (p.223)
- Morning sea kayak (p.219)
- Lunch in Bar Harbor (p.221)
- Afternoon hike up the Precipice (p.172).
- Or, if the Precipice is closed, hike up Cadillac Mountain's West Face Trail (p.186)
- Late afternoon swim at Echo Lake (p.247)
- Dinner in Southwest Harbor (p.247)

    *Alternate outdoor adventure: Rock climbing (p.28)

ONE PERFECT RAINY DAY

It's true! It's possible to have fun on Mount Desert Island even if it rains.

- Breakfast wherever, whenever
- Midmorning trip to the Bar Harbor Oceanarium (p.217)
- Late-morning trip to the Dorr Museum of Natural History (p.217)
- Lunch in Bar Harbor (p.221)
- Afternoon trip to any Bar Harbor museum (p.216)
- Afternoon shopping in Bar Harbor
- Dinner wherever, whenever
- Evening movie in Bar Harbor (p.220)

at a glance

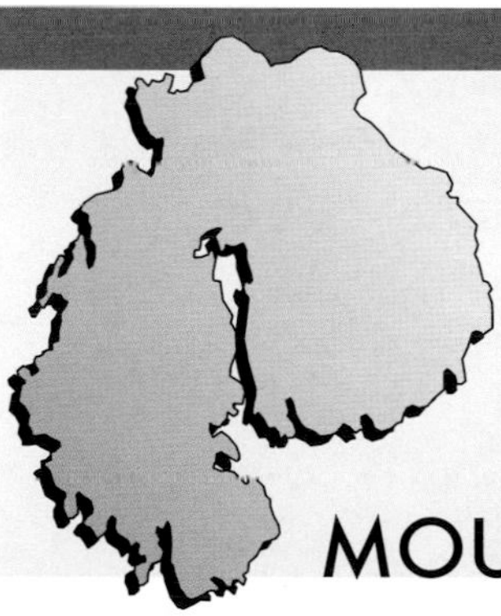

Area: 108 square miles
Length: 16 miles
Width: 10 miles
Mountain Peaks: 26
Lakes and Ponds: 28

MOUNT DESERT ISLAND

MOUNT DESERT ISLAND
Cuisine

Lobster

Maine is home to the tastiest, most succulent lobster on the planet, hauled up fresh daily. Don't even think about visiting Mount Desert Island without sampling Maine's quintessential crustacean. After all, lobster meat is virtually fat free, has fewer calories and less cholesterol than chicken or beef, and is full of vitamins A, B12, E, *and* Omega-3 fatty acids. While there are plenty of restaurants that serve up expensive, multicourse lobster dinners on Mount Desert Island, some of the best lobster is also some of the least expensive, served at lackluster shacks where the emphasis is on nothing more than the freshest lobster possible. Don't be fooled by appearances! These temples of seafood are as good as it gets.

Best Authentic Lobster Meal: Thurston's Lobster Pound (p.251). Located in the remote town of Bernard. Like any genuine lobster mecca, Thurston's is a bit rough around the edges, but the waterfront views and fresh lobster can't be beat.

Second Best Authentic Lobster Meal: Beal's Lobster Pound (p.247). Located in Southwest Harbor. Another diamond in the rough, but the minimalist setting hardly matters once the lobster hits your mouth.

Best Lobster Dish: Lobster strudel, Cafe Bluefish (p.221). One of the tastiest entrees in Maine.

Worst Lobster Dish: Ben & Bill's Lobster Ice Cream (Bar Harbor). One of the most appalling foods you'll ever put in your mouth.

Wild Blueberries

Over 90 percent of the wild blueberries sold in the U.S. are harvested within 60 miles of Mount Desert Island. In addition to being delicious, wild blueberries contain twice the antioxidants of their cultivated cousins, and studies indicate that blueberries help improve memory.

Best Blueberries: growing wild along Acadia's hiking trails. Keep your eyes out.

Best Blueberry Pancakes: Cafe This Way (p.221)

Best Blueberry Drink: Bar Harbor Blueberry Ale, brewed by the Atlantic Brewing Company.

Local Brews

Bar Harbor is said to have more microbreweries per capita than any other town in the United States. And while that only translates to three breweries (the town has a rather small capita), all three are fantastic. There's nothing like finishing a hard day of hiking or kayaking with a frosty, local microbrew. My personal favorite: Atlantic Brewing Company's Bar Harbor Real Ale.

Atlantic Brewing Company
The largest brewer on the island. Offers free tastings every half hour and tours of their brewhouse three times daily. Located on Knox Road between Route 3 and Route 102. Open seven days a week. 207-288-2337, www.atlanticbrewing.com

Bar Harbor Brewing Company
This small husband-and-wife brewery is famous for their award-winning Cadillac Mtn. Stout. Free tours & tastings, June–Sept. 135 Otter Creek Rd, Route 3, Bar Harbor, 207-288-4592, www.barharborbrewing.com

Maine Coast Brewing Company
A traditional English-style brewery offering a wide selection of handcrafted beers and seasonal brews. Free tours and tastings. 102 Eden Street, Route 3, Bar Harbor, 207-288-4914, www.bhmaine.com/brewery.html

OUTDOOR ADVENTURES

HIKING

Acadia has over 130 miles of incredible hiking trails—so many that I devoted an entire chapter to them (p.169).

BIKING

The best biking on the island is found along the carriage roads (p.195). You can also bike the Park Loop Road (p.107), but the heavy automobile traffic can be a pain in the summer. Bike rentals are available at several shops in Bar Harbor (p.219).

SEA KAYAKING

The rugged coast of Maine is one of the best places to sea kayak in America, and the region around Mount Desert Island is one of the best places to sea kayak in Maine. Several Bar Harbor companies offer sea kayak rentals, guided day trips, and multiday tours featuring camping or overnight stays at coastal inns (p.219). Overnight trips will probably set you back a couple hundred dollars, but if you love sea kayaking there's no better way to spend your money.

ROCK CLIMBING

Mount Desert Island's bold, dramatic cliffs make it one of the few places on the East Coast where you can rock climb directly above the ocean. If you've never rock climbed before, two outfitters in Bar Harbor offer lessons: Acadia Mountain Guides Climbing School (198 Main Street, 207-288-8186, www.acadiamountainguides.com) and the Atlantic Climbing School (24 Cottage Street, 207-288-2521, www.acadiaclimbing.com). If you're an experienced rock climber, pick up a copy of *Acadia: A Climber's Guide* by Jeff Butterfield.

CROSS-COUNTRY SKIING

When heavy winter snow blankets Mount Desert Island, Acadia's carriage roads (p.195) offer some of the best cross-country skiing in Maine. Ski equipment is rented and sold at Cadillac Mountain Sports in Bar Harbor (p.220).

Otter Cliffs

SWIMMING

There are two ocean beaches on Mount Desert Island—Sand Beach (p.123) and Seal Harbor Beach (p.228)—but entering the bone-chilling water often borders on masochism. Your best bet for a swim that doesn't induce shock is Echo Lake, located just north of Southwest Harbor. The southern end of the lake has a small, man-made beach (popular with families), while Echo Ledges, located at the base of the Acadia Mountain parking area on Route 102, is a more secluded spot where you can jump off small rocky ledges into the water.

SCENIC FLIGHTS

Nothing puts Acadia's bold topography in perspective like a scenic flight around Mount Desert Island. Island Soaring offers Cessna flights and motorless glider flights departing daily from the Hancock County/Bar Harbor Airport in Trenton. They also offer lighthouse flights and custom trips along the Maine coast (207-667-7627, www.islandsoaring.net).

Champlain Mountain

GEOLOGY

MOUNT DESERT ISLAND is the most stunning geologic feature on the eastern seaboard. Unlike most of the East Coast, which is sandy and flat, Mount Desert Island towers 1,500 feet above a rocky shore. No fewer than 26 mountain peaks rise above the island, some visible up to 60 miles out at sea. How these mountains formed is a fascinating story that involves colliding continents, erupting volcanoes, scouring glaciers, and countless other splendid catastrophes. The result of all this turmoil: one of the most beautiful islands in the North Atlantic.

Five hundred million years ago, Maine was covered by an ancient ocean that predated the modern Atlantic. Geologists refer to this ocean as the Iapetus Ocean (Iapetus was the father of Atlas, "Atlantic"). As ancient rivers flowed into the Iapetus Ocean, vast amounts of sediment accumulated offshore. This sediment—a combination of sand, mud, and silt—piled up in thick layers, and over millions of years the bottom layers were compressed into sedimentary rock. As tectonic plates shifted, this newly formed rock was pushed deep below the surface of the Earth where extreme heat and pressure metamorphosed it into schist (a metamorphic rock similar to slate). The schist that formed is called Ellsworth schist, and it is the oldest rock found on Mount Desert Island. After the Ellsworth schist formed, tectonic action pushed it to the surface where it became the floor of the Iapetus Ocean. As rivers deposited fresh sediments into the Iapetus Ocean, a new layer of sedimentary rocks formed on top of the Ellsworth schist called the Bar Harbor Formation. A few million years later, ash from erupting volcanoes settled on top of the Bar Harbor Formation to form a third set of rocks: the Cranberry Isles Series.

By 350 million years ago, the three oldest rocks on Mount Desert Island—Ellsworth schist, Bar Harbor Formation, and Cranberry Isles Series—had formed. At this point all three rocks were part of an ancient continent called Avalonia, lying somewhere between North America and Europe in the Iapetus Ocean. But slowly, as tectonic plates shifted, North America and Avalonia started moving toward each other. Several million years later, the two continents collided. The collision pushed up a chain of mountains that were perhaps as high as today's Rocky Mountains and sent huge pools of magma rising up under the previously formed Avalonian rocks. When the rising magma reached the layers of Ellsworth schist, Bar Harbor Formation, and Cranberry Isles Series, it stopped rising and cooled into granite, creating the fourth (and most famous) rock formation on Mount Desert Island. But all four rocks were still buried deep underground.

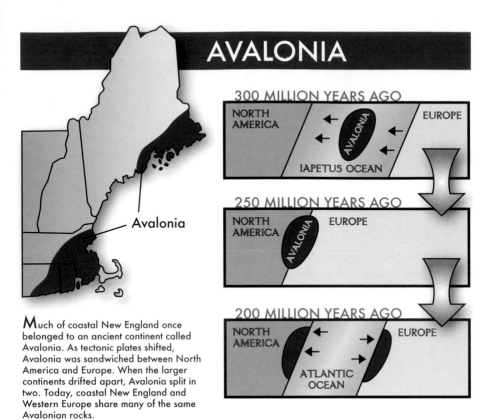

AVALONIA

300 MILLION YEARS AGO
NORTH AMERICA — AVALONIA — EUROPE — IAPETUS OCEAN

250 MILLION YEARS AGO
NORTH AMERICA — AVALONIA — EUROPE

200 MILLION YEARS AGO
NORTH AMERICA — ATLANTIC OCEAN — EUROPE

Avalonia

Much of coastal New England once belonged to an ancient continent called Avalonia. As tectonic plates shifted, Avalonia was sandwiched between North America and Europe. When the larger continents drifted apart, Avalonia split in two. Today, coastal New England and Western Europe share many of the same Avalonian rocks.

Although geologists know a good deal about rock formation on Mount Desert Island between 500 and 300 million years ago, the last 300 million years are a bit of a mystery. Any evidence indicating what kind of landscape existed here has long since eroded away. They do know, however, that about 70 million years after the collision of North America and Avalonia, Africa and Eurasia smashed into North America to form a huge, supercontinent called Pangea (a collision that also pushed up the Appalachian Mountains). Maine was located near the geographic center of Pangea—a position close to the equator that created a warm, tropical climate.

Then, around 200 million years ago, North America and Europe broke away from Pangea and started to drift apart. Avalonia split in two, with the eastern portion stuck to North America and the western portion stuck to Europe. (Even today, coastal Maine and Western Europe share many of the same Avalonian rocks.) As North America and Europe drifted apart, the Atlantic Ocean was born and North America moved north from the equator to its present location. During this time erosion slowly chipped away the landscape to reveal the rocks that would ultimately form Mount Desert Island. But it would take one last dramatic act of geology before the island took on the familiar profile we know today.

THE ICE AGE

Around 2.4 million years ago, Earth entered the Ice Age and thick layers of snow accumulated in the arctic that compacted into massive sheets of ice. Soon the ice sheets were set into motion under the pressure of their own weight, at which point they became glaciers. Pushing south, the glaciers consumed everything in their path. Boulders, soil, trees—everything but the bedrock was picked up and carried along. But even the bedrock did not escape unscathed. The glaciers, essentially dirty ice full of loose debris, acted like giant sheets of sandpaper, grinding down the bedrock and smoothing it out. The glaciers advanced over much of North America, then retreated abruptly. Then they advanced and retreated again. Then they advanced and retreated 15 more times. The most recent glacial cycle ended 12,000 years ago.

Scientists are unsure what triggered the Ice Age (a period we are still in today) or why glacial advance has followed a somewhat predictable cycle. One culprit seems to be a small wobble in the earth's orbit that affects how much solar radiation reaches the Earth. When the wobble goes one way, solar radiation increases, temperatures rise, snowfall decreases, and the glaciers melt. When the wobble goes the other way, solar radiation decreases, temperatures drop, snowfall increases, and the glaciers advance. This cycle—earth wobbling, glaciers advancing, Earth wobbling, glaciers retreating—generally lasts about 120,000 years. Cool periods of glacial advance last about 100,000 years, with warmer, interglacial periods of about 10,000 to 20,000 years in between. (We are currently about 15,000 years into the current interglacial period.)

The last period of glacial advance started about 100,000 years ago. By about 20,000 years ago, massive glaciers had reached the coast of Maine. At the time, Mount Desert Island was home to a series of jagged granite mountains separated by deep, V-shaped valleys that had been cut by streams over millions of years. (It should be noted that by this point Mount Desert Island was no longer an island; so much ocean water was frozen in the glaciers that sea levels had dropped, exposing much of the coast and connecting the

> During the last Ice Age, North America was covered with 1.5 times more ice than is found on Antarctica today.

island to the mainland). The glacier flowed into the V-shaped valleys and gouged them out into graceful U-shaped valleys. Soon only jagged mountain peaks stuck out of the glacier like rocky islands in a sea of ice. As the glacier continued to advance, even the peaks disappeared under the ice.

At the glacier's maximum extent, Mount Desert Island was buried under several thousand feet of ice. The glacier covered every mountain in New England, stretched 200 miles past the present shoreline, and reached as far south as Long Island. So much of the world's water was frozen in glaciers that global ocean levels dropped as much as 300 feet. And the tremendous weight of the glacier (one cubic mile of ice weighs 4.5 billion tons) compressed the land 300 feet below present-day levels.

Then, around 18,000 years ago, Earth's temperatures rose and the glacier started to melt. Within 5,000 years the glacier had retreated as far as central Maine. Three thousand years later it had disappeared from the state entirely. The melting glacier released massive amounts of water, forming huge rivers that raced to the sea and cut deep channels into the land. (Those channels now form the major rivers that flow through Maine.) As water returned to the sea, ocean levels rose, flooding the compressed land and sending saltwater up to 60 miles inland in Maine. On Mount Desert Island, only the highest peaks remained above water. But free of the weight of the glaciers, the compressed land slowly rebounded and rose back toward its original levels, draining the interior of the state and forming the present shoreline. The weight of the glaciers was so extreme that parts of Maine are still rebounding today, roughly 14,000 years later.

Before the glacier arrived, the coast of Maine was covered in sandy beaches—the result of waves grinding down a once rocky shore. But when the glacier descended it pushed the sand out to sea and permanently tilted the land near the coast, which was covered in hills before the Ice Age. When ocean levels rose, those tilted hills, scraped bare by the glacier, formed the hundreds of rocky inlets and bays that now make up the present shoreline.

Today, elements such as rain, ice, and waves continue to chip away at Mount Desert Island. Some geologists estimate that erosion removes about two inches from the island every 1,000 years. A million years from now, the forces of geology will have rendered Mount Desert Island completely unrecognizable to modern eyes. In the meantime, it remains one of the most beautiful places in the world.

MOUNT DESERT ISLAND ROCKS

Ellsworth schist: The oldest rock on the island. Dark green or gray coloration. Often has swirls like marble cake, the result of twisting deep underground.

Bar Harbor Formation: Named for its excellent exposure along the Bar Harbor shoreline. Dark gray in its natural state, but weathers to a tan or lavender color. Erodes to form jagged edges and flat slabs.

Cranberry Island Series: The least common rocks in Acadia. Generally light gray to blue-gray in color. Good examples are found on the Cranberry Isles.

Granite: The most common rock on the island, visible on any mountain peak. Light gray with a pinkish hue. There are three types of granite on Mount Desert Island, each distinguished by the size of its mineral crystals.

ICE AGE GLACIERS

At the peak of the last Ice Age, North America was covered by an enormous glacier several miles thick in places. Mount Desert Island was buried under several thousand feet of ice, which was so heavy that it compressed the land. At the glacier's maximum extent, it stretched roughly 200 miles into the Gulf of Maine.

North America
18,000 years ago

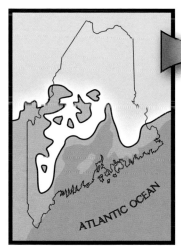

13,000 years ago

As temperatures on Earth continue to rise, the glacier continues its retreat. Melting ice causes sea levels to rise, flooding the compressed land in Maine.

11,000 years ago

Free of the weight of the glaciers, the land in Maine rebounds and drains. But with so much ocean water still trapped in retreating glaciers, sea levels remain below present levels.

White-tailed Deer Fawn

ECOLOGY

FROM AN ECOLOGICAL standpoint, Acadia is one of the most diverse national parks in America. With elevations ranging from sea-level to 1,500 feet, a location at the boundary of two of North America's major botanical zones, and a landscape filled with forests, lakes, and wetlands, Acadia is home to an astonishing number of plants and animals. All told, over 50 species of mammals, 320 species of birds, and 1,000 species of flowering plants have been identified in the park (as well as hundreds of sea creatures in the waters offshore). Even more amazing, Acadia's species are all found on less than 48,000 acres. Outside of a tropical rainforest, there are few places in the world with so much natural diversity packed into such a small space.

Mount Desert Island lies at the boundary of North America's northern boreal forest (found in northern Maine and Canada) and eastern deciduous forest (found in southern Maine and southern New England). The boreal forest is dominated by evergreens such as spruce and fir, while the deciduous forest contains oak, maple, and other hardwoods that burst with color in the fall. In all, over 30 different species of trees are found on Mount Desert Island, including pitch pines growing at the northeastern limit of their range and jack pines growing at the southern limit of their range. Scattered among the trees are over 40 kinds of shrubs and hundreds of smaller plants such as wildflowers, mosses, and ferns.

Hike up the island's tallest mountains and the forests soon give way to rocky peaks. Here, small populations of alpine plants scrape out a living in tiny pockets of soil. Because there is so little vegetation on the mountain peaks, there is very little soil development—a self-reinforcing process that prevents larger plants like trees from taking root. Lying exposed at high elevations, the peaks experience cooler than average year-round temperatures. This creates an excellent habitat for several rare species of plants normally found much farther north, including Alpine clubmoss and mountain sandwort (notable for its tiny white flowers).

During the summer, the island's mountains are often bathed in thick fog, providing moisture for the plants at the top. Any rain that falls tends to rush off the peaks immediately because there is so little vegetation to absorb the water or slow it down. As the water cascades down the rocks it often forms dozens of temporary waterfalls. The water then gathers into dozens of streams and flows into the island's lakes, ponds, and marshes.

Roughly 20 percent of Acadia is considered wetland. Because wetlands attract plants

Joe Hanlon

Beech Mountain

and animals from both land and water, they are extremely important to the park's ecology. Wetlands also provide stopover points for birds migrating on the Atlantic flyway. In fact, Mount Desert Island is considered one of America's premier birding locations. (James Audubon, founder of the Audubon Society, did much of his research here.) Lying on the boundary of North America's temperate and sub-arctic zone, the island attracts a spectacular range of birds that flock here in the spring to feast on the 6,500 species and subspecies of insects so far recorded in the park. By winter, however, the island's bird population has been reduced to a fraction of its summertime high.

Not surprisingly, Mount Desert Island is also home to a wide range of mammals. Some, such as snowshoe hares and white-tailed deer, are strict vegetarians, nibbling on grasses and shrubs. Others, such as red foxes and eastern coyotes, are predators that feed on smaller animals. Acadia also contains 11 of Maine's 19 amphibian species, including the thumbnail-sized spring peeper frog, whose chirp echoes throughout wetlands in the spring. But because Mount Desert Island is located so far north, there are few reptiles, which are cold-blooded and prefer a warmer climate. Only two species of turtle and five species of snake are found in the park (none of the snakes are poisonous).

In addition to land on Mount Desert Island, Acadia National Park also includes many smaller offshore islands. Characterized by cool climates and rocky terrain, these islands feature a habitat similar to Mount Desert Island's mountain peaks, well suited to sub-arctic plants and animals normally found much farther north. The lack of predators on many offshore islands also provides excellent breeding sites for seabirds.

Cadillac Waterfall

MARINE ECOLOGY

Perhaps the most fascinating aspect of Acadia's ecology is the Gulf of Maine, a shallow region (on average 500 feet deep) that covers 69,000 square miles of the Atlantic Ocean from Cape Cod to Nova Scotia. About 200 miles offshore lies the Gulf's most prominent physical feature: Georges Bank. Only 13 feet deep in places, George's Bank is a shallow ridge that acts as a barrier between the Gulf and the open Atlantic. Five major rivers flow into the Gulf of Maine, depositing an average of 250 *billion* gallons of nutrient-rich freshwater each year. Georges Bank helps retains this freshwater to create, in effect, a massive estuary (a place where freshwater and saltwater mix that is extremely biologically productive).

In addition to the freshwater deposited by rivers, cold ocean water from Nova Scotia is cycled into the Gulf of Maine via the Labrador Current. Because cold water contains significantly more dissolved oxygen and carbon dioxide than warm water, it helps form the foundation of a thriving food chain. Taken together, the estuary-like quality of the Gulf and the cold water flowing down from Nova Scotia have created an ecosystem teeming with life. The Gulf of Maine is often referred to as the richest offshore fishery in the world.

The Gulf's food chain begins with phytoplankton, tiny plants that drift along the sunlight-rich surface of the ocean. Phytoplankton are then fed upon by tiny animals called zooplankton. (The name plankton is derived from the Greek *planktos* "to wander" because these small organisms float wherever the current takes them). The green, murky water found in the Gulf is visual evidence of the abundant phytoplankton, which are fed upon by barnacles, crabs, and fish such as herring and mackerel. The plankton-eating fishes are then fed upon by fish-eating fishes such as tuna and sharks, as well as marine mammals like seals and porpoises. During the summer, when plankton and fish are most abundant, migrating whales arrive in the Gulf to feast on the natural bounty. Humpback, finback, and minke whales can all be seen in the waters offshore Mount Desert Island.

GEORGES BANK

During the last Ice Age, glaciers extended roughly 200 miles into the Gulf of Maine. At the front of the glaciers was a vast accumulation of rocks and debris called a terminal moraine. When the glaciers retreated, the terminal moraine was left behind. At the start of the glacier's retreat, ocean levels were roughly 200 feet below present-day levels, and the terminal moraine created a gravelly ridge connected to the mainland. But as the massive glaciers melted, ocean levels rose and flooded the terminal moraine, creating the shallow underwater ridge now called Georges Bank. (Another part of the terminal moraine, Cape Cod, remains above water.) From time to time, fishing trawls on Georges Bank have dragged up mammoth bones, remnants of the Ice Age creatures that roamed there when it was connected to the mainland.

Meanwhile, groundfish such as haddock and cod, crustaceans such as lobsters and crabs, and dozens of other strange and wonderful sea creatures dwell on the floor of the Gulf year-round.

Although tides rise and fall an average of three to six feet over much of the Earth, on Mount Desert Island tides rise and fall an average of 11 feet. Farther north in Canada's Bay of Fundy, which branches off of the northern tip of the Gulf of Maine, tides fluc-

Pound for pound, the world's oceans produce more plants each year than the continents. Phytoplankton alone absorb significantly more carbon dioxide than the rainforests and produces 70 percent of the world's oxygen.

tuate an astonishing *50 feet*—the largest tidal fluctuation in the world. These dramatic tides are caused by what's commonly called the "bathtub effect." For a variety of reasons, water in the shallow Gulf of Maine sloshes back and forth like water in a bathtub. The cycle of this sloshing happens to coincide with the natural cycle of the tides, amplifying them dramatically. (The funnel-like shape of the Bay of Fundy amplifies the tides even more.) Such large tides help stir to up nutrients in the Gulf, further boosting ecological productivity.

Tides occur twice daily in the Gulf of Maine, with two high tides and two low tides about every 24 hours and 50 minutes. Tides are caused by the gravitational pull of the moon, which creates a bulge in the Earth's ocean water. The sun also exerts a gravitational pull on the ocean, but it's much smaller than the pull of the moon. When the earth, sun, and moon are arranged in a straight line, at each full and new moon, the tides rise higher and fall lower than they normally do. (Such tides are called "spring" tides because they *spring* higher.) When the sun and the moon line up at right angles to each other, in the quarter phases, they counteract each other's gravitational pull, creating a small tide known as a "neap" tide. (The word neap is based on a Scandinavian word meaning "hardly enough.") On Mount Desert Island, spring tides and neap tides boost and lower tides an additional three to four feet.

INTERTIDAL ZONE

When people think of marine ecology, they often picture fish, whales, and other creatures of the open sea. But between the ocean and the land lies another amazing ecosystem: the intertidal zone. This dramatic region, encompassing the shore between high and low tide, is a world onto itself. Creatures living here have adapted to a brutal environment where they must cope with life above and below water, tolerate extreme temperature fluctuations, and survive the violent pounding of the waves (which can produce pressures up to 500 pounds *per square inch*). Some of the most dynamic organisms on the planet are found in the intertidal zone, but much of this amazing landscape remains

INTERTIDAL ZONE

Encompassing the shore between high and low tide, the intertidal zone is home to some of the park's most fascinating plants and animals

Splash Zone or Black Zone: Splashed by waves and spray at high tide, but never fully submerged. Called the Black Zone because of a black-colored algae that grows on the rocks.

Barnacle Zone: Easily identified by presence of tiny white barnacles.

Rockweed Zone: Home to large strands of rockweeds such as knotted wrack and bladder wrack. As the tide rises, tiny air bladders in the rockweeds lift them toward the surface where they can better photosynthesize. At low tide, rockweeds provide moist protection for mussels and other intertidal creatures.

Irish Moss Zone: A loosely defined zone that often overlaps with the zones above and below it. Its namesake plant, Irish Moss, has beautiful iridescent tips and grows in small, dense clumps.

Kelp Zone: Home to some of the intertidal zones most famous creatures, including starfish, sea urchins, and sea cucumbers. A thick curtain of moist kelp protects all of these animals at low tide.

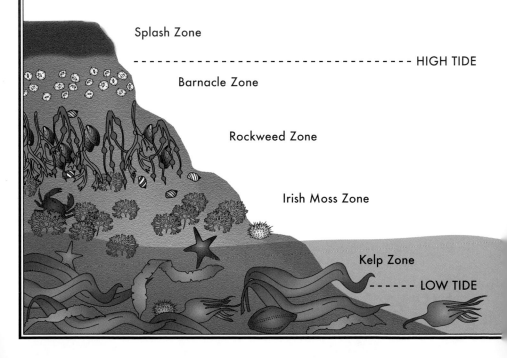

Splash Zone

--------------------------------------- HIGH TIDE

Barnacle Zone

Rockweed Zone

Irish Moss Zone

Kelp Zone

- - - - - LOW TIDE

STARFISH

Found in the lower intertidal and subtidal zones. Starfish grow up to eight inches across and come in a rainbow of colors. They are famous for their ability to regrow lost arms. Starfish use their arms to pry open shellfish such as mussels.

DOG WHELK

Found in the upper and mid-intertidal zones. Easily identified by its pointed, often-banded spiral shell. Dog whelks feed on barnacles by climbing on top of them and forcing their valves open. To feed on mussels they use a tongue-like organ called a radula to drill a hole into the mussel's shell. They then ingest their victims from the inside out.

SEA CUCUMBER

Found in the lower intertidal and sub-tidal zones. Growing up to 10 inches long, sea cucumbers have leathery skin and five rows of tube feet. They ingest sand and other sediments and filter out nutrients. When seriously threatened, sea cucumbers can disgorge their internal organs to confuse predators. The organs will later regenerate.

SEA URCHIN

Found in the lower intertidal and sub-tidal zones. Urchins have a spiny, limestone shell to protect their soft internal organs from predators. Seagulls often drop urchins on rocks from the air to crack open their hard shells.

ROCK CRAB

Found in the lower intertidal and sub-tidal zones. Rock crabs range from Canada to South Carolina. They grow up to five inches wide and are named for their rock-like appearance. Like many intertidal animals, rock crabs can regrow lost appendages.

off limits to the public because so much of the Maine coast is privately owned. In Acadia National Park, however, over 40 miles of rocky shoreline are open to visitors, revealing the wonders of this fascinating ecosystem. And due to the Gulf of Maine's large tides, Acadia's intertidal zone is particularly dramatic.

Near the top of the intertidal zone you'll find organisms that live most of their lives above water. Organisms at the bottom of the intertidal zone, meanwhile, spend most of their lives underwater, and they will die if exposed to the air for too long. In between these two extremes lies a wide range of plants and animals adapted to specific amounts of time above and below water.

As the tide rises and falls, tidepools form in the crevices of craggy rocks. These temporary pockets of water are filled with life-forms as small as plankton and as large as starfish and sea anemones. The location of a tidepool within the intertidal zone has a dramatic effect on the plants and animals that can live there. Tidepools at the top of the intertidal zone experience drastic fluctuations in temperature, water level, and salinity as sunlight heats the pool and water evaporates throughout the day. Tidepools at the bottom of the intertidal zone, however, are exposed for much shorter periods of time, and their fluctuations are much less severe.

HUMAN IMPACT

As European settlement spread throughout coastal Maine in the late 1700s, settlers altered the environment in many significant ways. Although Indians had been altering the environment for centuries through hunting, harvesting, and intentional fires to clear brush, their activities—limited by small populations and a lack of technology—had a relatively minor impact on the land. But when European settlers arrived, their impact was swift and dramatic.

Perhaps the most obvious change was to the forest. Lumbering was a vital component of the early economy of coastal Maine; oaks, cedars, and chestnuts were all harvested for shipbuilding and other construction. The most important tree, however, was the white pine, which grows up to 250 feet high and towers above all other trees in New England. White pines were perfect for ship's masts, and no tree of comparable height grew anywhere in Europe. Until the 1630s, England was forced to import timber from

European Settlers introduced (intentionally and unintentionally) many European plants and animals to New England. Among the non-natives: dandelions, black flies, cockroaches, and honeybees.

Baltic forests, then splice the boards together to make masts. The white pines of New England (referred to as "skyscrapers" before steel buildings snagged the name) rescued England from its reliance on foreign timber and gave a profound boost to the British

Bar Harbor, late 1800s

navy. But aggressive harvesting soon wiped out the limited white pine population that once thrived along the Maine coast.

While some loggers pushed farther north and west in search of white pines, others turned their attention to cedars and white oaks, which were used for building materials and fuel. But it was farmers who had the greatest impact on the land, clearing out huge swaths of forest to graze cattle. By the mid-1800s, large sections of Mount Desert Island had been completely stripped of trees. As farming declined over the past century, however, island trees have reclaimed much of their former territory.

Human activities also took a huge toll on animal populations in coastal Maine. As trade between Indians and Europeans increased in the 1600s, Indians hunted animals in much larger quantities than their pre-contact lifestyles required. Soon, many animals, particularly beaver, had been hunted out of much of the region. Later, coastal residents began to hunt seabirds for their meat, eggs, and feathers. But because seabirds reproduce in such small numbers, hunting had devastating effects. One species, the flightless, penguin-like great auk was hunted to extinction. Unable to fly away from humans, great auks were simply rounded up on shore and clubbed to death. Ultimately public pressure, including the founding of the National Audubon Society, encouraged protection of the remaining seabird population. The landmark Migratory Bird Treaty Act of 1918 banned seabird hunting, and many bird sanctuaries were established along the coast of Maine. Over time, many seabird populations have slowly recovered.

On Mount Desert Island, roughly 250 years of human settlement has also taken its toll in other, more subtle ways. Today nearly one-quarter of the plants found in Acadia are non-native "exotics." Free from the diseases and pests that keep their populations in check back home, some exotics have thrived in Acadia. Purple loosestrife, a beautiful European plant with magenta flowers that bloom in July and August, has flourished in wetlands throughout the park, muscling out native plants and sending ripples through the food chain. Within the boundaries of Acadia, purple loosestrife populations are kept under strict control, but outside the park the plant is thriving. About a dozen other non-native species are currently considered a disturbance to the park's native ecosystem.

But the ecosystem most in peril these days is the Gulf of Maine. Once-abundant fish such as cod, haddock, swordfish and bluefin tuna have seen their populations plummet over the past century due to overfishing. In the 1960s, modern technology allowed fish

Each year, over a billion pounds of seafood are harvested from the Gulf of Maine.

catches to skyrocket, and for the first time harvesting capacity exceeded available stocks. At one point roughly 300 fishing ships, mostly from Eastern Europe, were taking over 310 million pounds of fish each year from the Gulf of Maine. To salvage the remaining stocks, the United States claimed jurisdiction over waters within 200 miles of shore, up from 12 miles in the 1940s.

With foreign competition removed, stocks were expected to surge, and the United States began offering subsidies to encourage domestic fishing. Their efforts were far too successful. By the early 1980s, domestic fishermen were hauling up even more fish than during the record catches of the 1960s. Not surprisingly, fish stocks again plummeted. In

WILD ATLANTIC SALMON

One of the most endangered (and controversial) species in Maine is the wild Atlantic Salmon. In the 1800s, the state's rivers were filled with hundreds of thousands of salmon, which spend their winters in the open Atlantic but return to Maine rivers each year to spawn (most notably in the Penobscot River, which empties into the Atlantic southwest of Mount Desert Island). Over the past century, however, wild salmon populations have plummeted due to overfishing, pollution, and (most significantly) dams, which limit their ability to spawn upstream. Although rivers are well stocked with salmon raised in hatcheries, wild salmon populations in Maine at one point fell to less than 2,000 fish.

In the late 1990s, conservationists launched a campaign to place wild Atlantic salmon on the Endangered Species List. The listing was publicly opposed by then-governor Angus King, who argued that so-called wild salmon, which had been breeding with farm-raised salmon for decades, were no longer a distinct species. The listing would place severe restrictions on eight major rivers, which, it was argued, would deal a significant blow to northern Maine's nascent salmon farming industry and blueberry farms, both of which relied on water from the rivers in dispute. In a region with a consistently below-average economy, salmon farming and blueberry farming are considered bright spots. Despite scattered local opposition, wild Atlantic Salmon was placed on the Endangered Species List in 2000. A lawsuit filed by groups opposing the listing was later dismissed in court.

1994 strict regulations governing catch limits, size requirements, and harvesting season were enacted to salvage the remaining populations. Government "buy-back" programs were also introduced to permanently remove fishing vessels from the Gulf—more tax dollars spent to fix a problem that tax dollars helped create.

Even today, stocks in the Gulf of Maine remain well below historical averages. And each year global demand for seafood continues to surge: bluefin tuna (prized for sushi) can fetch up to $80,000 per fish; a sea urchin plucked off Mount Desert Island can be served as an appetizer in a Tokyo restaurant the next night; and every two weeks a jet loaded with 200,000 pounds of lobster flies from Bangor, Maine to Paris, France. Although lobster populations appear to be doing fine, urchin harvests have declined 85 percent over the last decade. Groundfish harvests (cod, haddock, flounder) have also plummeted, dropping 75 percent over the past two decades.

Despite strong opposition from the $650 million dollar New England fishing industry, parts of the Gulf have been shut down to fishing in recent years. Georges Bank experienced highly publicized closures in 1994, resulting in a swift upswing of certain species, most notably herring. But only one of the eighteen species of groundfish has fully recovered from overfishing. And drag trawling, in which massive nets are dragged along the ocean floor to snare groundfish (a process that has been compared to clear-cutting), continues unhindered over much of the Gulf. On average, every inch of the Gulf of Maine is dragged over by groundfishing equipment each year.

Sustainable yields in the Gulf of Maine are possible in the long-run, but only with much needed changes to the centuries old fishing traditions that have become outdated in modern times. Hopefully, as the public becomes more aware of the issues facing the Gulf of Maine, such changes will soon become a reality.

AMERICAN LOBSTER

Homarus gammarus

No seafloor in the world has a higher concentration of lobsters of than the Gulf of Maine. Young lobsters start out with two claws of equal size, but as they mature they develop a preference for one claw or the other. The preferred claw becomes the crusher claw, which is larger, more powerful, and used to crush prey such as muscles and clams. The other claw becomes the shredder claw, which is used to seize and cut. If a lobster loses a claw or any other appendage it will regenerate over time. Lobsters grow throughout their life, and in rare cases they can reach lengths exceeding 4 feet. To make room for their expanding body lobsters must frequently shed (or molt) their shell, much like a snake sheds its skin. Prior to a molt, a lobster drains calcium out of its shell and stores it to be recycled in the new shell. After a molt, a lobster's Jell-O-like muscles are completely exposed. The lobster eats its old shell to absorb additional calcium and then seeks shelter while it waits for its new shell to harden. In a lobster's first five years, it will molt roughly 25 times, gaining 15 percent body length and 50 percent volume each time.

U.S. RANGE

Found from Maine to North Carolina

INFO

Max. Length: 4+ feet

Max. Weight: 40+ pounds

Lifespan: 75+ years

Total Population: Unknown

Avg. ME Catch: 25 million lbs.

ATLANTIC PUFFIN

Fratercula arctica

Petit Manan Island, about 14 miles north of Mount Desert Island, marks the southern limit of the Atlantic puffin's range, which stretches across the North Atlantic from Maine to France. Puffins live on the open ocean for most of the year, waddling onto land only to breed and raise chicks from April to August. Puffins are amazing swimmers, using their wings to "fly" underwater and their feet to steer. While underwater they hunt small fish and can carry dozens in their beak at one time. (A puffin was once seen carrying 62 fish in its beak!) In Maine, puffins were over-hunted by early settlers for food and feathers. By 1900 only one isolated colony remained. In the 1970s, hundreds of puffin chicks were taken from Newfoundland (where strong puffin populations remain) and reintroduced to the Gulf of Maine. Since then puffins have recolonized a handful of offshore islands. The Atlantic puffin's scientific name, *Fratercula arctica*, means "little friar of the north," a reference to the black and white plumage that resembles a friar's robe.

U.S. RANGE

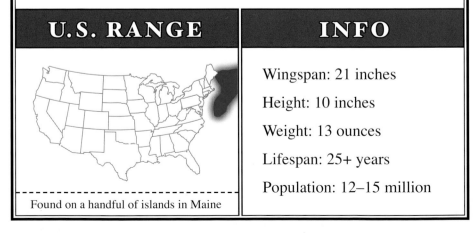

Found on a handful of islands in Maine

INFO

Wingspan: 21 inches

Height: 10 inches

Weight: 13 ounces

Lifespan: 25+ years

Population: 12–15 million

BALD EAGLE

Haliaeetus leucocephalus

Bald Eagles range over much of North America, but in Maine they are found mostly along the coast where they can prey on seabirds. At one time there may have been as many as 75,000 bald eagles in the lower 48 states, but by the early 1960s there were fewer than 900. Hunting and habitat loss had eliminated bald eagles throughout much of their natural range. In 1967 bald eagles were placed on the federal Endangered Species List. Since then, the birds have made a remarkable comeback. There are now roughly 30,000 bald eagles in the lower 48 states and an additional 40,000 in Alaska. In Maine, however, bald eagles are still listed as an endangered species. Although bald eagles range over a vast territory, most return to nest within 100 miles of where they were raised. Nests are reused year after year and are added to annually (some can reach up to 10 feet across and weigh up to 2,000 pounds!). Bald eagles do not develop their distinctive white head until their fourth or fifth year. "Bald" is derived from an old English word meaning white. The bald eagle's scientific name means "white-headed sea eagle."

U.S. RANGE

Nests along the shore in Acadia

INFO

Wingspan: 7 feet

Length: 40 inches

Weight: 14 pounds

Lifespan: 30 years

Population: 70,000

BEAVER

Castor canadensis

Beavers are the largest rodents in North America. They use their large incisors to gnaw away at the trunks of trees, then drag the fallen logs to streams to build dams. Because beavers store food underwater, they require a deep pond that won't fully freeze in the winter, allowing them access to their food. Dams are built out of logs, sticks, and rocks cemented together with mud. The resulting pond creates prime wetland habitat for beavers and many other animals. Once a dam is built, beavers construct a living space known as a lodge by heaping together a separate pile of debris and then gnawing out a roomy chamber from the bottom up. Beavers use their long flat tails as rudders, allowing them to steer while towing logs in the water. On land, beavers use their tail to prop themselves up as they gnaw on trees. The beaver's double fur coat, which is so thick that water never touches a beaver's skin, was prized by early trappers, and throughout the 1700s and 1800s beavers were hunted extensively. By 1900 beavers had been removed from much of their natural range, including Mount Desert Island. Protective laws and reintroduction programs were later enacted, and beaver populations slowly began to recover. Beavers were successfully reintroduced to Acadia in 1920.

U.S. RANGE

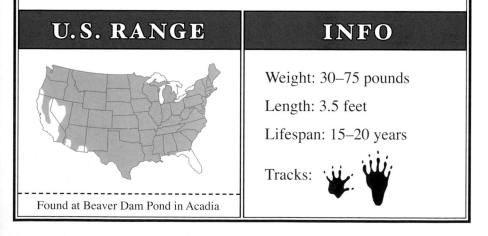

Found at Beaver Dam Pond in Acadia

INFO

Weight: 30–75 pounds

Length: 3.5 feet

Lifespan: 15–20 years

Tracks:

COMMON EIDER DUCK

Somateria mollissima

The common eider is the largest duck in the northern hemisphere, and the most commonly spotted duck near Mount Desert Island, often seen flying in a low formation over the ocean. Eiders are extremely social and sometimes travel in flocks of up to 1,500. Their breeding range extends from Maine to the Arctic, but eiders rarely nest on Mount Desert Island, preferring the solitude of smaller offshore islands where they lay eggs in a nest made out of down plucked from the mother's body. Sometimes mothers bring their young to the shores of Mount Desert Island to feed, but the journey is a treacherous one. Along the way, chicks can be killed by a variety of predators, including seals, gulls, hawks, and fish. Adult eiders feed primarily on shellfish, swallowing mussels and crabs *whole* (muscles in eider stomachs are specially designed to crush shellfish and digest both the shell and its contents.) In the 1800s eiders were harvested for their soft down, which was used in pillows and quilts. When populations plummeted, a harvesting ban was enacted to protect the remaining birds. Since then, coastal Maine has seen a comeback in common eider populations.

U.S. RANGE

Found offshore Mount Desert Island

INFO

Wingspan: 3 feet

Length: 24 inches

Weight: 5 pounds

Population: 2 million

COMMON LOON

Gavia immer

Famous for their haunting call, loons are among the most ancient flying birds alive today. They first appeared 60 million years ago and have remained virtually unchanged since then. Unlike most flying birds, loons have solid bones that enable them to dive up to 150 feet. Their bright red eyes are capable of seeing at depths below 15 feet and their three-toed feet are located far back on their body for maximum speed in the water—a feature that makes them extremely awkward on land. (Most scholars believe the word *loon* is derived from the Scandinavian word "lom," meaning clumsy person.) While under water loons pursue fish and other prey with their dagger-like bills. Adult loons mate for life, and partners spend each summer at the same nesting site. Winters are spent at separate locations on the coast, but partners are reunited in the spring to mate. Female loons usually lay two olive green eggs with dark spots. Chicks take to the water almost immediately after hatching, and can sometimes be seen riding on their parents' backs.

U.S. RANGE

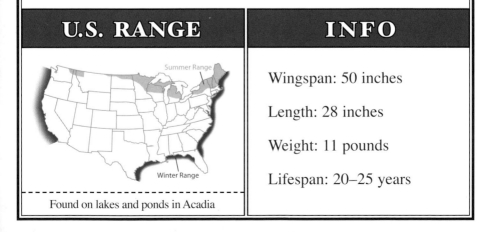

Summer Range

Winter Range

Found on lakes and ponds in Acadia

INFO

Wingspan: 50 inches

Length: 28 inches

Weight: 11 pounds

Lifespan: 20–25 years

HARBOR SEAL

Phoca vitulina

Harbor seals are commonly spotted basking on small offshore islands. They can dive up to 500 feet, stay under water for up to 30 minutes at a time, and eat up to 10 percent of their body weight per day. During low tide seals spend hours on exposed rocks and ledges—basking, sleeping, scratching, and yawning. During high tide they forage for fish and squid in the water. Seal pups, born in the spring, are able to dive within minutes of birth, and they sometimes hitch a ride on their mother's back by holding on with their flippers. But after only a few weeks mothers abruptly abandon their young. About one-third of pups die during their first year, victims of storms, disease, and predation by ospreys, black-backed gulls, and sharks. Adult harbor seals are solitary at sea, but they gather by the dozen on shore. In the late 1800s, fishermen blamed seals for damaging their nets and depleting their catches. A bounty of $1.00 per seal was offered in Maine to reduce populations. By the early 1900s, harbor seals had disappeared from much of the coast with no noticeable change in fish catches or net damage. The bounty was repealed in 1905, and since then populations have slowly recovered.

U.S. RANGE

Found on Egg Rock in Frenchman Bay

INFO

Length: 5 feet

Weight: 150–200 pounds

Lifespan: 30 years

Population: 500,000

HUMPBACK WHALE

Megaptera novaeangliae

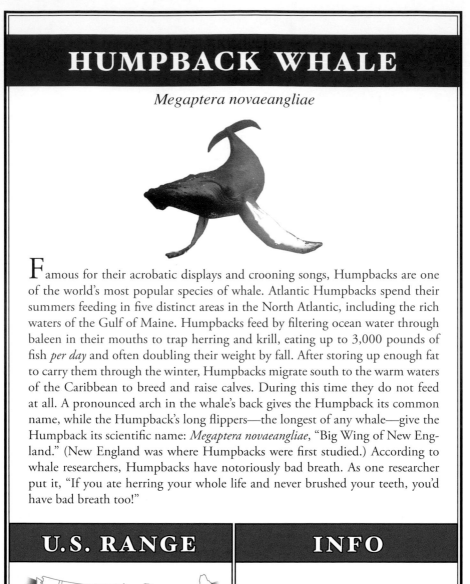

Famous for their acrobatic displays and crooning songs, Humpbacks are one of the world's most popular species of whale. Atlantic Humpbacks spend their summers feeding in five distinct areas in the North Atlantic, including the rich waters of the Gulf of Maine. Humpbacks feed by filtering ocean water through baleen in their mouths to trap herring and krill, eating up to 3,000 pounds of fish *per day* and often doubling their weight by fall. After storing up enough fat to carry them through the winter, Humpbacks migrate south to the warm waters of the Caribbean to breed and raise calves. During this time they do not feed at all. A pronounced arch in the whale's back gives the Humpback its common name, while the Humpback's long flippers—the longest of any whale—give the Humpback its scientific name: *Megaptera novaeangliae*, "Big Wing of New England." (New England was where Humpbacks were first studied.) According to whale researchers, Humpbacks have notoriously bad breath. As one researcher put it, "If you ate herring your whole life and never brushed your teeth, you'd have bad breath too!"

U.S. RANGE

Found 25 miles offshore Mt. Desert Island

INFO

Length: 55 feet

Weight: 90,000 pounds

Lifespan: 50 years

Population: 12,000–15,000

PEREGRINE FALCON

Falco peregrinus

Peregrine falcons are birds of prey that can spot victims from thousands of feet above. Once a target is selected, a peregrine will dive bomb it at speeds topping 200 mph. The collision creates an explosion of feathers, and victims that don't die immediately upon impact have their necks broken by the peregrine's specially designed beak. Peregrines are such successful strikers that they were used to kill Nazi carrier pigeons in World War II. By the early 1970s, however, peregrine falcons were at the brink of extinction. Hunting, habitat loss, and the extinction of the passenger pigeon (an important source of food) had reduced the worldwide population to less than 40 pairs. To save the remaining birds, young peregrines were raised in captivity and released in the wild. In 1984 peregrine chicks were introduced to Acadia, and the first successful nesting occurred in 1991. Since then peregrines have returned to Acadia each year to raise three or four chicks. Although Maine populations remain low, the captive breeding program has been remarkably successful overall. In 1999 peregrines were removed from the federal Endangered Species List. There are currently over 1,650 breeding pairs in the United States and Canada.

U.S. RANGE

Nest on Precipice, Jordan Cliffs in Acadia

INFO

Wingspan: 41 inches

Length: 16 inches

Weight: 1.6 pounds

Lifespan: 15 years

Population: 3,300

RACCOON

Procyon lotor

A common myth holds that raccoons always wash their food before they eat it. But these beady-eyed bandits are hardly that dignified. Raccoons eat just about anything they can get their hands on—clean or dirty—including frogs, birds, fruits, nuts, worms, slugs and garbage. They are especially ravenous in the fall, increasing their body fat up to 50 percent to prepare for the lean winter months. Although raccoons prefer wooded areas near streams, they have adapted remarkably well to urban environments, traveling along sewage pipes and living in attics and chimneys. Famous for the black "mask" that covers their face, raccoons are intelligent, crafty creatures. Their eyes are incredibly well adapted to darkness, allowing them to carry out mischievous deeds at night such as removing trash lids and prying open coolers to steal food. Despite their cute and cuddly appearance, raccoons have a nasty disposition and a tendency to carry rabies, so they should never be approached. The name raccoon is derived from the Algonquian *arakunem*, "one that scratches with its hands." Other tribes have similar names for raccoons that refer to the animal's nimble hands.

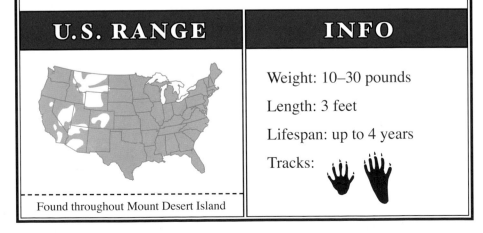

U.S. RANGE

Found throughout Mount Desert Island

INFO

Weight: 10–30 pounds

Length: 3 feet

Lifespan: up to 4 years

Tracks:

RED FOX

Vulpes fulva

Sleek and swift, crafty and cunning, red foxes have captivated wildlife watchers throughout the world. Highly adaptable, their range includes North America, Europe, Asia, North Africa—even Iceland and Japan. Although a member of the dog family, foxes display many feline characteristics such as stalking, pouncing, and toying with wounded prey. They also have elliptical cat-like eyes, which can narrow to a slit to give them exceptional vision in bright light. In addition, a reflective membrane at the back of the eye causes light to pass over the retina twice, giving them excellent night vision. Their superior vision, combined with ears that are sensitive enough to hear mouse footsteps under snow and a sense of smell that is 100 times greater than that of humans, makes them highly skilled hunters. Foxes eat virtually anything they can catch including grasshoppers, crickets, small birds, squirrels, rabbits, and lizards. Mothers often bring partially dead animals back to the den for the pups to play with to sharpen their survival skills. While still less than a month old, pups fight among themselves to establish dominance. The more dominant pups are fed first by the parents.

U.S. RANGE	INFO

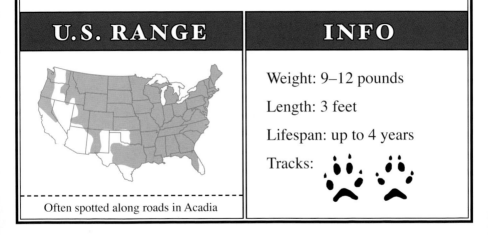

Often spotted along roads in Acadia

Weight: 9–12 pounds

Length: 3 feet

Lifespan: up to 4 years

Tracks:

SNOWSHOE HARE

Lepus americanus

Snowshoe hares are masters of disguise. In the summer they sport a grayish brown coat that helps them blend in with grasses and shrubs. As winter approaches, shorter days trigger a biological response that turns their coat almost entirely white, providing excellent camouflage in the snow. Snowshoe hares are preyed upon by foxes, coyotes, owls, and hawks. When the hare senses a predator, it freezes to avoid detection. If necessary it can flee at speeds up to 30 mph, hopping 12 feet in a single bound and making sharp zigzags to confuse predators. Snowshoe hares often spend their days sleeping in hidden locations, becoming active only at night or in the low light of dawn or dusk. They mate and give birth year-round, with females producing up to eight young per litter, up to four times per year, and young hares running within hours of birth. The populations of snowshoe hares are highly cyclical, becoming extremely plentiful every 10 years or so, then plummeting dramatically. The cause of this phenomenon is not fully understood, but it may have to do with unsustainable population densities. Researchers have studied some areas that contain up to 10,000 snowshoe hares per square mile.

U.S. RANGE

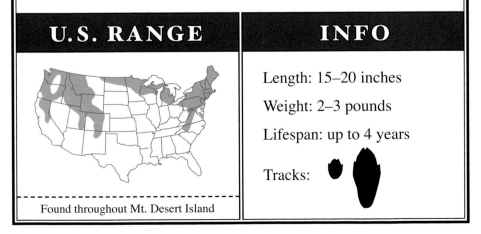

Found throughout Mt. Desert Island

INFO

Length: 15–20 inches

Weight: 2–3 pounds

Lifespan: up to 4 years

Tracks:

WHITE-TAILED DEER

Odocoileus virginianus

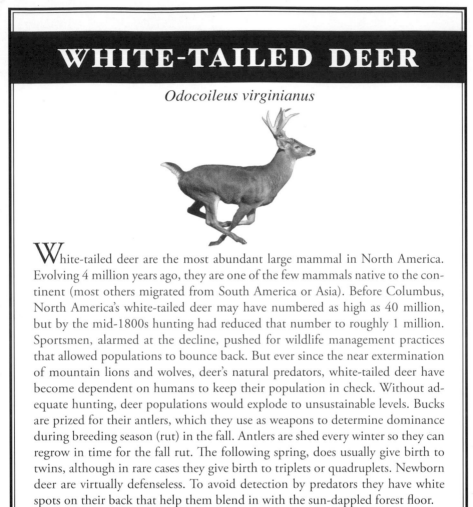

White-tailed deer are the most abundant large mammal in North America. Evolving 4 million years ago, they are one of the few mammals native to the continent (most others migrated from South America or Asia). Before Columbus, North America's white-tailed deer may have numbered as high as 40 million, but by the mid-1800s hunting had reduced that number to roughly 1 million. Sportsmen, alarmed at the decline, pushed for wildlife management practices that allowed populations to bounce back. But ever since the near extermination of mountain lions and wolves, deer's natural predators, white-tailed deer have become dependent on humans to keep their population in check. Without adequate hunting, deer populations would explode to unsustainable levels. Bucks are prized for their antlers, which they use as weapons to determine dominance during breeding season (rut) in the fall. Antlers are shed every winter so they can regrow in time for the fall rut. The following spring, does usually give birth to twins, although in rare cases they give birth to triplets or quadruplets. Newborn deer are virtually defenseless. To avoid detection by predators they have white spots on their back that help them blend in with the sun-dappled forest floor.

U.S. RANGE	INFO

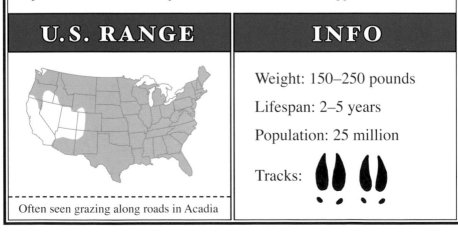

Weight: 150–250 pounds

Lifespan: 2–5 years

Population: 25 million

Tracks:

Often seen grazing along roads in Acadia

Passamaquoddy man

HISTORY

NOT LONG AFTER glaciers retreated from New England, humans settled the land. Around 10,000 years ago, pre-Indian hunters arrived in Maine and scraped out a living on the tundra left in the glacier's wake. At the time, Ice Age creatures such as six-foot long beavers and possibly mammoths and mastodons roamed the inland regions. The hunters chased game throughout the interior of the state, but it wasn't until about 5,000 years ago that the coast of Maine was settled. By that point temperatures had warmed, the Ice Age mammals had become extinct (most likely due to overhunting), and the modern ecology of Maine had taken shape.

Maine's Indians are collectively known as the Wabanaki, a group that includes the Penobscot, Passamaquoddy, Micmac, and Maliseet tribes. *Wabanaki*, loosely translated, means "People of the Dawn" due to Maine's eastern location—one of the first places in North America to see the rising sun. The Wabanaki were highly mobile, moving seasonally to take advantage of various plants and animals. They paddled canoes along the state's waterways, and established temporary villages along the banks of rivers and the coast.

Of the four Wabanaki tribes, the Penobscot and the Passamaquoddy are the two most closely associated with Mount Desert Island. They called the island *Pemetic*, "Mountain Range," and some Wabanaki spent their winters there to take advantage of the ocean's warming effect.

On Mount Desert Island the Wabanaki diet was rich in seafood. The men fished haddock and bass, and hunted seals and porpoises from birch bark canoes. At night, they sometimes paddled over a mile offshore to hunt sturgeon by torchlight. Women collected clams, mussels and other shellfish near the shore. (The Passamaquoddy word for Bar Harbor was *Man-es-ayd'ik*, "Clam-Gathering Place.") Women were also responsible for cooking, cleaning, and other daily chores.

On land the Wabanaki supplemented their diet with plants and game, including deer, bear, caribou, and moose. In the winter they chased game on snowshoes, which allowed them to move quickly across deep snows that slowed their prey down. Although agriculture was practiced in eastern Maine, it was never relied upon.

Micmac man, 17th century

Maine's growing season is very short, so only a handful of crops such as corn, beans and tobacco were cultivated in the warm summer months.

By 1600, when the first Europeans arrived, there were an estimated 32,000 Wabanaki living in Maine and Canada (about 41 people per 100 square miles). European explorers were fascinated by the Wabanaki. As one visitor noted, "I should consider these Indians incomparably more fortunate than ourselves ... their lives are not vexed by a thousand annoyances ... They mutually aid one another in their needs with much charity and without selfseeking. There is a continual joy in their wigwams." Another observer claimed that the Wabanaki "start off to their different places with as much pleasure as if they were going on a stroll ... for their days are all nothing but pastime."

Although Europeans did not settle the Maine coast until the mid-1700s, European contact had an immediate impact on Wabanaki life. In the early 1600s, a European fad for beaver pelt hats decimated beaver populations in Europe, and trappers soon eyed North America's abundant beaver supply. With demand running high, Indians such as

One early European explorer noted that the Wabanaki, "have no beards, the men no more than the women ... They have often told me that at first we seemed to them very ugly with hair both upon our mouths and heads; but gradually they have become accustomed to it, and now we are beginning to look less deformed."

the Wabanaki were eager to trade pelts for metal tools, guns, and alcohol. But as trading with Europeans increased, the Wabanaki began to abandon their traditional self-sufficient lifestyle in favor of the international marketplace.

At the same time, previously unknown European diseases such as smallpox and influenza, to which North American Indians had no natural immunity, ravaged Wabanaki communities. In 1618 alone, a massive plague killed nearly three-quarters of the native population of coastal Maine. With their communities decimated by disease and warfare, many Wabanaki abandoned their traditional religious beliefs and converted to Christianity.

By the mid-1800s, the Wabanaki population had fallen to less than a thousand individuals. As white settlers poured into Maine over the coming decades, the remaining Wabanaki lost access to much of their traditional territory, including Mount Desert Island. It wasn't until Bar Harbor became a popular resort town in the late 1800s that some Wabanaki returned, camping in tents and selling traditional Indian crafts to tourists.

EUROPEAN DISCOVERY

Some historians believe Vikings were the first Europeans to visit the coast of Maine. Others have speculated that European fisherman secretly fished Maine's waters long before Columbus set sail. (Some even believe that prior to 1492 Columbus overheard fisherman on the docks of Bristol, England discussing North America, thus inspiring his historic voyage.) But the first recorded voyage to Mount Desert Island comes from Giovanni De Verrazano, who led a French expedition to the New World in 1524.

Searching for a northern passage to Asia, Verrazano landed at present-day North Carolina and named it "Archadia" based on a mythical landscape described by the Greek poet Virgil. He then sailed north to explore the rest of the coast. When Verrazano reached Maine he encountered the Wabanaki, whom he described as, "of such crudity and evil manners, so barbarous, that despite all the signs we could make, we could never converse with them." As Verrazano's boat approached the shore the Wabanaki yelled and shot arrows at them. The Indians, however, were eager to trade with the Europeans for metal tools—albeit with the aide of a basket on a line shuttled safely between the ship and the shore. When Verrazano's ship departed, the Wabanaki sent them off by "exhibiting their bare behinds." Verrazano returned the favor by naming the Maine coast *Terra Onde di Mala Gente*, "Land of Bad People."

The Wabanaki's less than hospitable "bon voyage" to Verrazano and their desire to trade for metal tools indicates that they had encountered Europeans before. But Verrazano was the first to map the region, mysteriously labeling a spot near Mount Desert Island "Oranbega."

Despite Verrazano's successful exploration, no settlement was attempted in New England for almost a century. Europe, preoccupied with wars at home and the plunder of Central and South America to the south, paid little attention to chilly, remote New

It's possible that the legend of Norumbega originated as a mistranslation of the Indian word for "wealth." While Indians viewed wealth in terms of natural resources like plants and animals, Europeans were quick to assume the word meant gold.

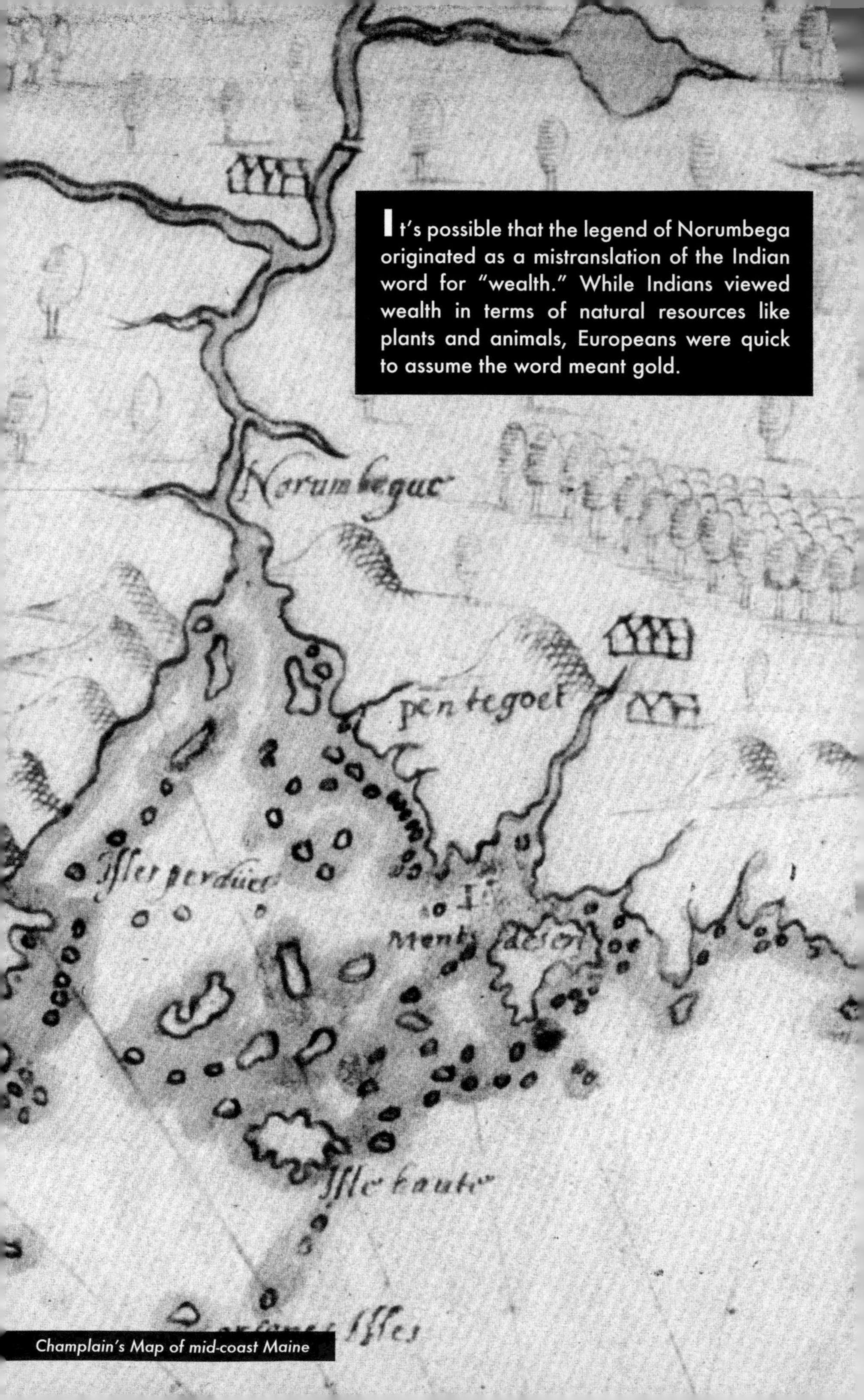

Norumbegue

pentegoet

Isles perdues

Ments deserts

Isle haute

Champlain's Map of mid-coast Maine

England. Although the rich waters off the coast of Maine were filled with fishermen by the late 1500s, they did little more than set up seasonal camps on offshore islands.

Before long, however, rumors of a fantastic city of gold located somewhere in Maine began to spread through Europe. The rumor is believed to have originated from a group of English sailors who were stranded in Mexico in 1567 and spent the next three years traveling on foot to New Brunswick, Canada. From there they hopped a fishing boat back to England and immediately hit the pubs, telling drunken stories of a fabulous city of gold located somewhere in Maine. They called the city "Norumbega"—a name strikingly similar to the *Oranbega* found on Verrazano's map.

In the mid-1500s, the idea of a golden city in Maine did not seem all that farfetched. Spain had hauled away enormous sums from the Aztecs and Incas, and it seemed only logical that more riches lay awaiting discovery in the New World. In 1579 and 1580, England sent two expeditions to mid-coast Maine to search for Norumbega. Although the expeditions failed to find the golden city, the British referred to the region between the Hudson River and the Bay of Fundy as Norumbega until 1606, when it was replaced by Virginia (which was then replaced by New England in 1620).

But England was not the only country with an eye on the region—and dreams of easy riches were not soon forgotten. In 1603, seventeen years before the Pilgrims landed at Plymouth Rock, France sent an expedition to North America led by Samuel Champlain. After landing at the mouth of the St. Croix River in Canada, Champlain sailed south to explore the coast of Maine. When he spotted the bald peaks of Mount Desert Island he noted in his log:

The island is very high and notched in places, so that there is the appearance to one at sea, as of seven or eight mountains extending along near each other. The summit of most of them is destitute of trees, as there are only rocks on them. The slopes are covered with pines, firs, and birches. I named it *L'isle des Monts-Desert* [Island of Barren Mountains].

SAMUEL CHAMPLAIN

Although earlier explorers had noticed the island before, Champlain was the first to give it a name. He was also the first to note that Mount Desert is, in fact, an island; previous maps had shown it connected to the mainland.

Continuing on, Champlain sailed up the Penobscot River, which empties into the Atlantic southwest of Mount Desert Island. If Norumbega did exist, he hoped to find it there. Champlain made his way as far as present-day Bangor where he found, to his dismay, nothing more than a simple Indian village. Frustrated, he concluded that the city of Norumbega was a myth. He did point out, however, that the region as a whole was "marvelous to behold."

By the time of Champlain's voyage, Verrazano's name for North Carolina, Archadia, had slowly migrated north on French maps. As Verrazano's map was drawn and re-drawn by countless map makers, Archadia became *L'Acadie* and began to refer to the region between Philadelphia and Montreal—a region that would soon become a major point of contention between the English and the French.

THE FRENCH JESUITS

Although there was no gold in Maine, the region was overflowing with natural resources. "The aboundance of Sea-Fish," wrote one early fisherman, "are almost beyond beleeving." Cod grew up to six feet in length and could be gathered by simply dropping a bucket into the water. Sturgeons were so numerous near the shore that they were considered a navigational hazard. The natural bounty was all the more dramatic compared with Europe's own depleted resources. And the items that Europe needed most—timber, cod, beaver, and sassafras (used to treat syphilis)—were among the most abundant in New England. For over a century Europe had virtually ignored the region. But once New England's natural resources were recognized, it began to look a lot more promising.

By the time of Champlain's voyage, both England and France claimed that *they* were the rightful owner of North America. But with no English settlements in the New World, and only a handful of French settlements in Canada, there were no actual conflicts over the land. Then, in 1607, England established a permanent settlement at Jamestown, Virginia. In response, France's Louis XIII granted North America to French noblewoman Antoinette de Pons, Marquise de Guercheville, who proposed a Jesuit mission on the coast of Maine.

In 1613 roughly 50 French Jesuits set sail from France, hoping to establish a settlement at the mouth of the Penobscot River. As they neared the coast of Maine they became surrounded by a thick fog. Unable to see more than a few feet ahead, the Jesuits grew terrified. If their ship ran aground it could easily sink, and they would be stranded with no supplies. Poor winds prevented the boat from retreating to deeper water, and the

The English warship sailed toward
Mount Desert Island, ready to attack...

helpless Jesuits simply gathered together and prayed. For two days their ship drifted aimlessly through the fog. When the fog finally lifted, the Jesuits found themselves staring at the eastern tip of Mount Desert Island.

Overjoyed, the Jesuits rowed to shore, raised a cross, and named the spot *Saint Sauveur*, "Holy Savior." Not long after they landed, they were approached by a group of Wabanaki Indians who encouraged them to stay on the island (presumably to benefit from the lucrative fur trade). But the Jesuits insisted they would continue to the mouth of the Penobscot. The Wabanaki then informed them that their leader, Sagamore Asticou, was mortally ill and wished to be baptized before he died. Eager to save a soul, the Jesuits climbed into the Indians' canoes and were paddled to the southern end of the island.

When the Jesuits met Asticou, they found him suffering from no more than a common cold. Many historians have since speculated that Asticou simply faked sickness to draw the Jesuits near and convince them to stay. If that was the case, it worked. Asticou was baptized and the Jesuits established their settlement near present day Southwest Harbor.

The Jesuits had only been on Mount Desert Island for a month when the King of England, eager to gain control of North America, ordered all French settlements south of present-day Canada destroyed. A 14-gun warship under the command of Samuel Argall was promptly dispatched from Jamestown, Virginia to carry out the King's orders. When Argall reached Penobscot Bay, he found a group of Wabanaki fishing among the offshore islands. The Indians, assuming the white men were friends of the French, tipped them off to the Jesuit's settlement. By the time they realized their mistake it was too late. Argall's ship sailed toward Mount Desert Island, ready to attack.

The Jesuits put up a weak fight, firing off only one shot before their settlement was laid to waste. Argall allowed a small group of Frenchmen to flee to Nova Scotia in an open boat, but the rest were taken to Jamestown as prisoners. The battle was one of the first skirmishes between the English and the French in North America. It would hardly be the last. For the next 150 years as the two countries battled over the region, Mount Desert Island became a virtual no man's land.

SETTLEMENT BEGINS

Ongoing battles between England and France kept many would-be settlers out of Maine until the late 1700s. During this time Mount Desert Island was used primarily as a navigational tool (on clear days Cadillac Mountain can be seen up to 60 miles out at sea). As one Englishman put it, the region north of the Penobscot River was, "a Countrey rather to affright then delight one, and how to describe a more plaine spectacle of desolation, or more barren, I know not." But shortly before the 1763 Treaty of Paris, which granted England control of New England, Mount Desert Island received its first permanent settlers.

In 1761, 22-year-old Abraham Somes sailed north from Gloucester, Massachusetts to Mount Desert Island to settle the town of "Betwixt the Hills" (later named Somesville). At the time, Mount Desert Island was owned by Francis Bernard, the royal governor of the Province of Massachusetts. Following the Revolutionary War, however, Bernard fled to England and the Americans confiscated his land. Bernard's son, who had sided with the Americans, ultimately petitioned the new government for his father's land, and being a good patriot he was granted it. But shortly after the transaction he sold the land and hightailed it back to England to join his father.

Not long after the Bernard incident, a French woman named Maria Teresa de Gregoire came forward and claimed that *she* was the rightful owner of Mount Desert Island. She traced her claim to her grandfather, Sieur de Cadillac, who had been granted the island a century earlier by the King of France. Although her claim was legally dubious, the new American government granted her the eastern half of the island as a show of good faith toward the French. De Gregoire and her husband moved to the island and opened a real-estate company, selling land at $5.00 dollars per 100 acres. (Because of the De Gre-

THE ORIGINAL CADILLAC

In 1688 a young French lawyer named Antoine Laumet swindled 100,000 acres along the coast of Maine that included Mount Desert Island. Undaunted by the violent land disputes in the region, the ambitious Laumet sailed to Mount Desert Island and changed his name to the noble sounding, yet completely fabricated, "Antoine de La Mothe, Sieur de Cadillac." Laumet also fabricated a noble-looking coat of arms to complement his new name. But Mount Desert Island offered little social mobility, and Cadillac headed west after only one summer. He later became the founder of Detroit, Michigan. Today, a modernized version of his fake coat of arms still graces the hood ornaments of millions of Cadillac automobiles.

Mount Desert Island sailors

goires, Mount Desert Island is the only place in the United States, other than Louisiana, where real estate titles can be traced back to the French Crown.)

By the late 1700s, fertile land near the coast was in short supply in southern New England, and ambitious settlers began heading north to the undeveloped harbors in Maine. Before long, Mount Desert Island was growing at a healthy clip. Initial development took place in Somesville, but settlement soon spread throughout the island. In 1796 the town of Eden (later named Bar Harbor) was incorporated. Fishing, shipbuilding, and lumbering were the primary occupations of the island's residents, who soon numbered several thousand, and for the most part they led peaceful, industrious lives. As one observer noted, "The women do the most of what there is in the way of farming, while the men, from early boyhood, are upon or in the water, chiefly as fishermen, but always as sailors, and unquestionably the best sailors in the world."

The island's economy revolved around the sea, and each day hundreds of sailboats could be seen plying the waters offshore. Local sailors shipped goods around the world, and many knew the coastlines of Europe and South America as well as they knew the coast of Maine. But sailing and fishing were rugged occupations. Men spent up to eight months of the year at sea, leaving their wives and children to fend for themselves at home.

Although Mount Desert Island continued to grow through the mid-1800s, access to the island from southern New England remained challenging. The journey was a multi-day affair that required a train ride to Portland, a steamboat cruise to Castine, and a schooner trip to Mount Desert Island. As a result, few people knew much about this remote, beautiful island. But following the arrival of a handful of landscape painters from New York, all that was about to change.

Fitz Hugh Lane, *Entrance of Somes Sound from Southwest Harbor*, 1852

THE HUDSON SCHOOL PAINTERS

In the mid-1800s, American cities faced immense growing pains. Overpopulation and the effects of the Industrial Revolution had transformed previously habitable cities such as Boston, New York, and Philadelphia into filthy, urban nightmares. Indoor plumbing had not yet been invented, and trash and human waste were left out in the street to rot. It's not surprising that during this time the art world experienced an overwhelming demand for landscape art. City dwellers, disgusted with the stink and grime of urban life, were desperate for wholesome scenes of unspoiled nature—hung conveniently on their townhouse walls. At the same time, railroads were creating an entirely new middle-class industry: tourism, which further fueled the demand for paintings of scenic destinations.

In 1844 Thomas Cole, America's leading landscape artist, traveled to Mount Desert Island and painted dramatic scenes of Sand Beach, Otter Cliffs, and Frenchman Bay. When Cole's work was exhibited in New York the following summer, it opened to mixed, but predominantly negative, reviews. One critic chided Cole for painting red rocks, noting, "the rocks are of a kind that no geologist would find a name for; the whole coast of Maine is lined with rocks nearly black in color." (In fact, the rocks on Mount Desert Island *do* have a reddish hue.) Another critic complained that, "the ocean appears like a vast cabbage garden."

Despite the poor reviews, Cole's paintings were a hit with the public, and a few years later his aspiring young student, Frederic Church, set off to create his own paintings of Mount Desert Island. Only 24 years old, Church was considered something of a prodigy. He spent his days exploring the island's rugged terrain and produced a series of dramatic

Sanford Robinson Gifford, *The Artist Sketching at Mount Desert, 1865*

the
Hudson River School

FREDERIC CHURCH

The painters of the Hudson River School not only introduced Mount Desert Island to the masses in the 1800s, but helped launch the American conservation movement. Two hundred years earlier, when the Puritans first arrived in New England, wilderness was viewed as a sinister, dangerous place—and back then it often was. The Puritans believed it was their moral duty to tame the land so religious communities could flourish. But even after the landscape had been tamed, their harsh view of nature persisted, and generations of Americans grew up viewing the frontier as nothing more than an obstacle to be conquered. But as more and more wilderness disappeared, a backlash developed.

Leading the charge were landscape painters such as Frederic Church and Thomas Cole, members of the Hudson River School of Art (which was not an actual *school* but an artistic movement). Cole rallied against the "apathy with which the beauties of external nature are regarded by the great mass, even of our refined community." Another artist declared, "Yankee enterprise has little sympathy with the picturesque, and it behooves our artists to rescue from its grasp the little that is left before it is for ever too late."

Artists of the Hudson School painted breathtaking scenes of the American wilderness that ignited the passions of the American public. They also used subtle visual techniques to convey their belief that wilderness was an extension *of* God, not an obstacle to His progress. One of their favorite tricks was to hide human features in the contours of rocks. This not only turned picture viewing into a kind of game, but also established a direct link between man and nature—and by extension God.

By portraying the American wilderness as a welcoming destination, the Hudson School hoped to dispel the notion that nature was an obstacle. They also wanted to prove that the American landscape was just as beautiful as Europe (and possibly more so), creating a much needed sense of national pride for the young democracy. On both counts, they succeeded. Hudson School exhibitions drew huge crowds and lured thousands of tourists to unique American destinations such as Mount Desert Island.

> " Yankee enterprise has little sympathy with the picturesque, and it behooves our artists to rescue from its grasp the little that is left before it is for ever too late. "

paintings that were received the following year with enormous success. In the days before television or photography, painting offered a rare glimpse of exotic destinations, and Church's stunning depictions of Mount Desert Island created a public frenzy. Thousands of people lined up outside of galleries in New York to view his work. Suddenly, Mount Desert Island found itself thrust into the national spotlight.

THE RUSTICATORS

Church's paintings generated a flurry of interest in Mount Desert Island, and before long both artists and tourists were making the multi-day journey to see the island first-hand. In the summer of 1855, Church returned to Mount Desert Island with 26 friends, a group that included artists, writers, businessmen, and their families. The group stayed at a Somesville tavern, spending their days hiking, fishing, sailing, picnicking, and otherwise thoroughly enjoying themselves. Although artists were present, the excursion was first and foremost a social expedition. What little drawing was done generally consisted of humorous sketches mocking one another. At the end of their month-long stay, the group threw a large party, inviting dozens of locals and importing a piano (the island's first) specifically for the event. Church held forth at the piano, indulging in his "perfectly inexhaustible" capacity for entertainment late into the night.

What seemed like nothing more than a deliriously satisfying summer actually set the tone for the first wave of visitors to Mount Desert Island. Later named Rusticators,

> " Now, most of the visitors to Mount Desert, even the prosaic folk, go prepared to enjoy the picturesque, the beautiful, the sublime. "

these early tourists—for the most part artists, professors and other intellectuals with leisure time on their hands—came to experience the simple pleasures of rugged coastal life. Rusticators required no fancy accommodations. They often rented out attic space from locals and paid for an extra spot at the family's dinner table. Locals, eager for some extra cash, were more than happy to accommodate the easy-to-please visitors, creating a wonderfully symbiotic relationship. An 1872 travel article in *Harper's Magazine* summed up the rusticator's lifestyle: "Now, most of the visitors to Mount Desert, even the prosaic folk, go prepared to enjoy the picturesque, the beautiful, the sublime."

During the day parties of several persons, ladies and gentlemen, start off on a walking expedition of five, ten, and fifteen miles to one or another of the many objects of interest on the sea-shore or up the mountains. There is a vigorous, sensible, healthy feeling in all they do, and not a bit of that overdressed, pretentious, nonsensical, unhealthy sentimentality which may be found at other places.

— *Harper's Magazine*, 1872

THE COTTAGERS

As stories, artwork, and magazine articles about Mount Desert Island continued to spread, interest in the island soared. But tourism was limited by the physical challenge of actually getting there. Few would-be tourists had the time, money or patience required for the multi-day journey. Then, in 1868, direct steamboat service was started between Boston and Mount Desert Island. A steamboat route drastically reduced the time it took to get to the island. It also dramatically increased the reliability of the voyage because travelers were no longer at the mercy of the wind. Within a few years, Mount Desert Island had become a major tourist destination.

Between 1868 and 1882, at least one hotel was built or thoroughly expanded on the island each year. The largest, Rodick House in Bar Harbor, contained over 400 rooms and boasted that it was the largest hotel in Maine. Locals welcomed the flood of cash, but some were left feeling a bit perplexed. When one visitor told a local innkeeper that, "It's the scenery we wish to see," the innkeeper replied, "Yes, I know, it's what them artist men come here for. But what it amounts to, after all their squattin' and fussin', I don't know."

If the innkeeper didn't already know, he was about to find out. In 1882 luxuries such as electricity and telephones arrived on Mount Desert Island, followed two years later by train service from Boston, which cut travel time to the island down to a single day. The

Bar Harbor's Kebo Club, late 1800s

result was predictable: the number of summer visitors quadrupled.

The tourist explosion quickly changed the face of Bar Harbor. As more and more wealthy visitors arrived, upscale development proceeded at a breakneck pace. Luxury hotels sprouted up in Bar Harbor farmland, and quaint general stores were replaced with boutiques showcasing the latest Parisian fashions.

Hoping to distance themselves from hotel life (which was becoming increasingly less exclusive), the wealthiest visitors built giant mansions along the shore. So as not to appear pretentious they referred to their gilded, servant-stocked fortresses as "cottages."

The community is now divided into two classes, one of which looks down upon the other.

The name fooled no one, however, and before long the social epicenter had shifted from hotel lounges to private dining rooms. The wealthiest families in America all added Bar Harbor "cottages" to their portfolio of mansions. The arrival of these prestigious families firmly cemented Bar Harbor's reputation as one of the most exclusive summer destinations in America. Among the richest of the rich, it was included as part of a spectacular year-long tour of resorts: Palm Springs in the winter, Newport in the spring, Bar Harbor in the summer, and the Berkshires in the fall.

In only a few short years, the tone of Bar Harbor had completely changed. It was no longer a place to relax and commune with nature; it had become a place to see and be seen. As longtime summer resident Edward Godkin put it, "The Cottager has become to the boarder what the red [squirrel] is to the gray, a ruthless invader and exterminator ... caste has been established ... the community is now divided into two classes, one of which looks down on the other." Such complaints were countered by the novelist F. Marion Barnes, who in 1896 declared that Bar Harbor was home to the finest conversation found anywhere in America. Despite the conflicting attitudes, the town's reputation as the gilded gateway to Mount Desert Island was firmly established, and visitors continued to arrive by the thousands.

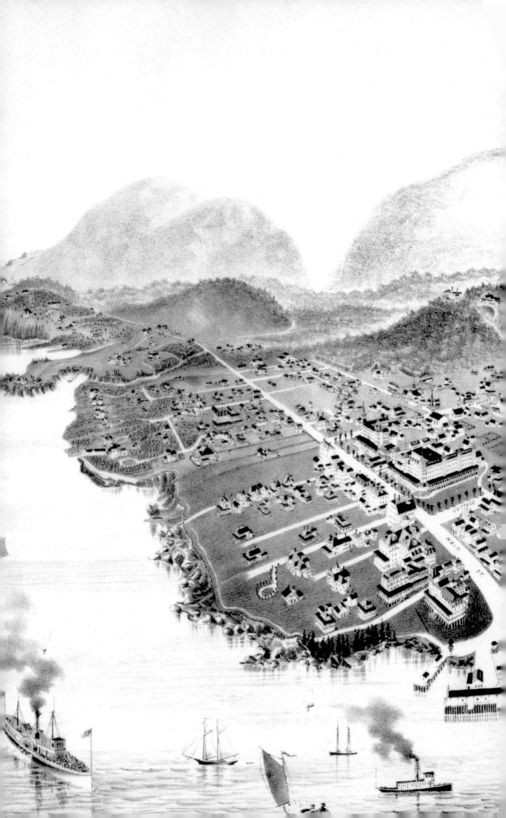

Bar Harbor, late 1800s

lost "cottages" of
BAR HARBOR

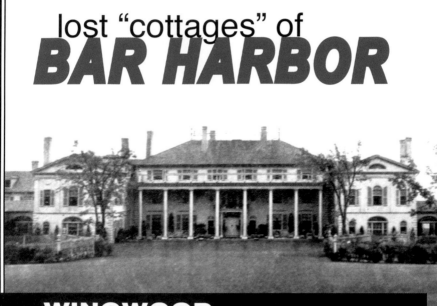

Bar Harbor Historical Society

WINGWOOD

Wingwood was the most extraordinary summer cottage in Bar Harbor. It belonged to Edward T. Stotesbury, who grew up poor in Philadelphia, started working at age 12, and eventually became a senior partner at J.P. Morgan & Company. In 1925, flush with cash, Stotesbury purchased a large mansion in Bar Harbor. His wife Eva took one look at the new property and promptly hired an architect. She ultimately spent over 1 million dollars remodeling the house. When the remodeling was complete, Wingwood boasted 80 rooms, 26 hand carved marble fireplaces, 52 telephone lines, and a 30 room servants wing. Some of Wingwood's bathrooms (28 total) featured gold fixtures, which Eva claimed were "economical" because "they saved polishing." Edward once remarked to his gardener that he would have been content with a small cottage and a supper of beans, but those beans would have to be eaten off of plates from one of Eva's two 1,200 piece dining sets. Eva's spending habits were legendary. She hired gardeners to move plants around Wingwood's grounds on a weekly basis, and employed a full-time fashion designer and "costume secretary." At one point Eva organized a $500,000 alligator safari to gather leather for a set of matching luggage. Following her death in 1946, Eva was remembered fondly as an exemplary hostess, one who "made every guest feel as if he or she were the only one invited." After the death of the Stotesburys, Wingwood fell into disrepair, and it was demolished in 1953.

CHATWOLD

Chatwold was the summer home of famed millionaire Joseph Pulitzer, by far the strangest cottager in the history of Bar Harbor. After earning a fortune in the newspaper business—where he introduced such revolutionary concepts as the daily sports page and the color comic strip—Pulitzer added Chatwold to his collection of mansions in New York, Georgia, and the French Riviera. His idiosyncrasies were legendary. Pathologically sensitive to noise, the sound of a nut cracking is said to have made him wince. When Pulitzer stayed in hotels he required the rooms above, below, and on either side of him to be kept vacant. To combat the irritating sounds of everyday life, Pulitzer spent $100,000 constructing the "Tower of Silence"—a massive granite structure on the right side of Chatwold that was designed to be 100 percent soundproof. The mansion also boasted the first heated swimming pool in Bar Harbor and a bizarre master bedroom that rotated on ball bearings.

Despite Pulitzer's legendary aversion to noise, he required a servant read him to sleep each night—and continue reading, in monotone, for at least two hours after he had fallen asleep. Legend has it that he would awake at the slightest change in pitch. Pulitzer also spent at least 12 hours a day in bed, dictating letters to his secretaries in a self-devised code that contained over 20,000 names and terms; Pulitzer was "Andes," Theodore Roosevelt was "Glutinous," and so on. Chatwold was ultimately demolished in 1945, several decades after Pulitzer's death.

JOSEPH PULITZER

ACADIA NATIONAL PARK

By the turn of the century, train service to Mount Desert Island had improved to the point where New Yorkers could hop a train in the morning and arrive in Bar Harbor later that evening. As more and more tourists flooded the island, some citizens grew alarmed at the speed of development taking place. Speculators were snatching up real estate, and the lumber industry, equipped with modern machinery, was eyeing the island's vast untouched forests.

Among the citizens most alarmed was former Harvard president and longtime summer visitor Charles Eliot. With the help of his friend, wealthy island resident Charles Dorr, the two men organized a group of private citizens dedicated to preserving Mount Desert Island for future generations. As savvy as they were civic minded, the Hancock County Trustees of Public Reservations (as they later came to be called) obtained a tax-exempt charter and quickly set to work purchasing land. Dorr enthusiastically took charge and acquired Eagle Lake, Cadillac Mountain, Otter Cliffs and Sieur de Monts Spring—all told over 6,000 acres.

Things were going well until 1913, when the Maine Legislature, under pressure from a variety of sources, attempted to revoke the Trustee's tax-exempt charter. Worried that the charter might ultimately be dissolved, Dorr suggested that the Trustees donate their land to the federal government. This was easier said than done. More government land meant more government spending, and Dorr was dispatched to Washington to convince lawmakers that land preservation on Mount Desert Island was worth the cost.

Using his considerable wealth and influence, Dorr pulled strings and cashed in on personal favors to arrange a meeting with President Woodrow Wilson. He also convinced the editors at *National Geographic* to publish an article about Mount Desert Island that generated tremendous public support for the cause. Two years later, a National Monument was created by Presidential Proclamation. Dorr's next move was to elevate the monument to national park status, which required an act of Congress. Despite the government's preoccupation with World War I, Dorr was able to gather the Congressional support he needed, and on February 26, 1919 Lafayette National Park was created. (The name Lafayette was chosen to reflect America's pro-French sentiment in the wake of the war.) Lafayette was the first national park established east of the Mississippi, and the first national park donated entirely from privately owned land.

Dorr became the park's first superintendent, at a salary of one dollar per year, and worked hard to expand Lafayette's holdings. In the late 1920s, a family of Anglophiles donated Schoodic Peninsula on the mainland with the stipulation that the name of the park be changed to something less French. And so, in 1929, Lafayette National Park became Acadia National Park. (Ironically, Acadia was based on an early French name for the region.) A decade later, the park acquired the southern half of Isle au Haut, a small island 15 miles south of Mount Desert Island.

the father of acadia
GEORGE DORR

Without George Dorr, Acadia National Park would not exist as we know it today. His tireless lobbying in Washington, D.C. was responsible for the creation of the park in 1919, and he devoted the rest of his life to preserving and expanding Acadia's holdings.

Dorr first visited Mount Desert Island in 1868 when his wealthy family purchased a summer home in Bar Harbor. As a young man, Dorr attended Oxford University and traveled extensively throughout Europe, exploring the Scottish highlands and hiking the Swiss Alps. When Dorr inherited his family's vast textile fortune at the turn of the century, he could have lived anywhere in the world he wanted. His choice: Mount Desert Island, where he could spend his days immersed in outdoor activities. When he wasn't hiking or biking across the island, he was hard at work building new trails and paths for such pursuits. Locals never ceased to marvel at his boundless energy and enthusiasm, which included a frigid morning swim off the Bar Harbor Pier each day until Christmas.

In 1944, at the age of 94, George Dorr died an impoverished man. He had spent his entire fortune, once valued at over $10 million, purchasing additional land for Acadia National Park. Toward the end of his life, shabby clothes replaced once expensive suits and he could not even afford to buy new books. Three years before his death, Dorr donated his family property to Acadia National Park. Reflecting on the gift where he had spent so many happy years, he wrote, "There is nothing in my work for the Island or the Park that I look back upon with greater satisfaction or sense of permanence."

Dorr died an impoverished man, having spent his entire fortune purchasing additional land for Acadia National Park.

THE GREAT FIRE OF 1947

By the time Acadia National Park was established, Bar Harbor was a town in decline. The Cottage Era had started to fade following the introduction of the personal income tax in 1913, and its fate was sealed with the stock market crash of 1929. By the late 1940s, many of Bar Harbor's once grand mansions had fallen into disrepair.

The next tumultuous chapter in the island's history began on a dry October day in 1947, a year in which a record drought engulfed the state. That summer and fall Maine received just 50 percent of its normal rainfall. By mid-October, Mount Desert Island was experiencing the driest conditions ever recorded. On October 17, at the height of the drought, a small fire broke out in the town dump north of Bar Harbor. Firefighters managed to control the blaze, but they were unable to completely put it out. When the fire started to grow, firefighters from across the state were dispatched to prevent a possible catastrophe.

For six days firefighters battled the stubborn blaze. Then, just when the fire was about to be declared out of control, gale force winds descended on Mount Desert Island, whipping up flames with 60 mph gusts. It was a nightmare scenario. At 4pm the fire covered 2,000 acres. Eight hours later, over 16,000 acres had burned. "It looked like two

Millionaire's Row, after the fire

gigantic doors had opened and towering columns of roaring flames shot down," recalled one firefighter. Many trees in the fire's path simply exploded as extreme heat pressurized their moist interiors.

Fueled by the howling winds, the fire raced along the northeastern shore of Mount Desert Island and approached Bar Harbor. A lucky shift in wind pushed the fire south, sparing the downtown section. But the destruction to the north of town and the fire that

> When all was said and done, the fire had burned over 17,000 acres on Mount Desert Island.

raged on to the south blocked all roads leading out of town. To evacuate the trapped citizens, fishermen from nearby towns were dispatched to the Bar Harbor town pier. Over 400 people escaped by boat before bulldozers cleared a path through the rubble north of town. Shortly thereafter, a caravan of 700 cars fled to safety along Route 3 as sparks from the lingering fire shot past their vehicles.

South of Bar Harbor the fire continued to rage, roaring around the eastern edge of the island with no signs of slowing down. As it approached Sand Beach, another lucky shift in wind pushed the fire to the tip of Great Head Peninsula. With winds pounding the inferno, flames leapt nearly a mile over the ocean, forcing nearby sailors to turn away to avoid igniting their sails. But confined to the peninsula, the fire's progress was finally contained.

On October 27, the fire was officially declared under control. But two weeks later, even after rain and snow had fallen, scattered fires continued to smolder below ground. On November 14, the fire was finally declared out. When all was said and done, the fire had burned over 17,000 acres (10,000 in Acadia) and caused five deaths. It had also destroyed nearly $20 million worth of property, including five hotels, 127 homes, and 67 mansions along once-fabled "Millionaires Row."

PRESENT DAY

As the wounds of the fire started to heal, the island took on a new character that defined it for the rest of the century. Although the fire destroyed much of Bar Harbor's gilded era, the island was no longer confronted with its reputation as a faded bastion of wealth. With Acadia National Park acting as its main draw, Mount Desert Island began to attract a new type of visitor: vacationing middle-class families. To accommodate the new arrivals, budget hotels and private campgrounds sprung up outside the park, and Bar Harbor reinvented itself as a sleepy tourist town. But as visitation increased year after year, the town grew increasingly less sleepy. Soon it had become one of the most popular summer destinations in New England.

Today the economy of Mount Desert Island revolves around tourism. Acadia National Park is tied with L.L. Bean's flagship store in Freeport, Maine as the state's most visited destination (about 3 million visitors annually), and each year over 80 cruise ships drop anchor in Bar Harbor. Although summer is the busiest season on the island, more and more visitors are arriving in the spring and fall, when the crowds are light and the

> ## Some have speculated that Mount Desert Island is entering a second Cottage Era...

weather is crisp and mild. Not so long ago, Labor Day was considered the end of the tourist season. Today, many hotels, shops, and restaurants remain open through October to accommodate the new crowds.

Although known first and foremost as a tourist destination, the island has also become a hotbed of scientific research. The Mount Desert Island Biological Laboratory studies cutting-edge marine biology, and Bar Harbor's Jackson Lab has become the largest mammalian research facility in the world. (Jackson Lab currently has over 1,200 employees, making it the largest employer in the region.) Meanwhile, Bar Harbor's College of the Atlantic, founded in 1969 with an emphasis on ecological studies, is home to 280 students who actively contribute to the intellectual pulse of the island.

But despite the down-to-earth incomes of scientists and professors—as well as fisherman, lobstermen, and local shopkeepers—real-estate prices have skyrocketed on the island in recent years as wealthy families have snatched up summer homes. With over 80 private jets touching down at the Bar Harbor Airport each Thursday in August, some have speculated that Mount Desert Island is entering a second Cottage Era. If that's the case, it's a Cottage Era with a distinctly different face. These days there's considerable social pressure from Old Money families, who have summered here for generations, to downplay wealth. Ostentatious displays are frowned upon; fleece is considered haute couture; and hiking and biking remain the distinguished activities of choice. For the moment, the emphasis remains on the good life, not the glam life.

But with so much money pouring into the island, gentrification has definitely taken hold—some of it much needed. Bar Harbor is no longer the nautical trinket capital of the world. Although a few aging novelty shops remain, they're slowly being edged out by outdoor retailers and upscale boutiques. Restaurants are also on the upswing, and Mount Desert Island is now considered one of the culinary hot spots of Maine. A number of sophisticated restaurants have opened in recent years, pushing the palate of the island distinctly forward.

But despite all the exciting changes, Mount Desert Island still continues to fly under the national radar, commanding nowhere near the same name recognition outside New England as Martha's Vineyard or Nantucket—two islands of comparable size yet seemingly unlimited fame. Given the geographical isolation of Mount Desert Island, it will probably remain continue to fly under the national radar for years to come. But only time will tell...

Schooner Head

ACADIA NATIONAL PARK

A S NATIONAL PARKS go, Acadia is posh. *Real* posh. The wealthy families that flooded the island in the late 1800s may have brought a lot of blue-blooded attitude, but they also brought a lot of cash. And when it came time to assemble Acadia National Park, no expense was spared. Hiking trails were paved with exquisite hand-cut stones; the Park Loop Road was designed by America's leading landscape architect; and John D. Rockefeller, Jr. personally commissioned a network of roads through Acadia for horse-drawn carriages ... *horse-drawn carriages!* (I told you this place is posh.)

Acadia's luxurious scenery is scattered in chunks along the rugged coast of Downeast Maine. The largest and most famous part of the park covers one-third of Mount Desert Island, but Acadia also includes Schoodic Peninsula (on the mainland), half of Isle au Haut (15 miles southwest), and about a half dozen tiny offshore islands. If you're only here for a weekend, focus your time on Mount Desert Island soaking in the park's most spectacular sights. If you're here for a week—or you've already explored Mount Desert Island—Schoodic Peninsula and Isle au Haut are definitely worth a visit, especially if you're looking to get away from the crowds (Isle au Haut is as close as you'll get to solitude in Acadia during July and August). Before you go anywhere, however, pick up a copy of the *Beaver Log*, available at any park visitor center. This free park publication lists current park openings/closures, ranger programs, tide schedules, sunrise/sunset times, and a wealth of other invaluable information.

On Mount Desert Island, the Park Loop Road is the undisputed highlight of the park. But dozens of pristine hiking trails would have made the park world-famous on their own. And it would be a sin to come all the way to Acadia and not explore the Rockefeller carriage roads. This delectable dilemma—what to do with so much good stuff at your fingertips—is what makes Acadia one of America's best national parks.

VISITOR CENTERS

Acadia's main visitor center (p.108) is located in Hulls Cove, just north of Bar Harbor. There's also the smaller Thompson Island Visitor Center, located just over the bridge connecting Mount Desert Island to the mainland (open late-May through mid-October, 10am–8pm). Off season you can visit park headquarters on Route 233, 3.5 miles west of downtown Bar Harbor (open daily 8am–4:30pm, except holidays).

ENTRANCE FEES

Acadia requires a pass at all times in any part of the park. A one-week pass costs $10 in season, $20 off season. There's also the annual Acadia pass ($40) or the annual national park pass ($50, good at all national parks). Passes can be purchased at the two park visitor centers, Blackwoods Campground, Seawall Campground, park headquarters, or the Bar Harbor Village Green.

RANGER PROGRAMS

Acadia offers over two dozen ranger-led programs, including hikes, nature walks, boat cruises, evening slide programs, short talks, and star gazing. Most are free but some require a fee. Check the *Beaver Log* for details.

PARK CONTACT INFO

Mailing address: Acadia National Park, PO Box 177, Bar Harbor, ME 04609
Telephone: 207-288-3338 (emergency: 911)
Email: acadia_information@nps.gov
Website: www.nps.gov/acad

FRIENDS OF ACADIA

Founded in 1986 to help preserve and protect Acadia National Park, Friends of Acadia has become a philanthropic powerhouse. Over the past two decades they've established two multimillion-dollar endowments—Acadia Trails Forever Program and the Carriage Road Endowment—and helped introduce the Island Explorer shuttle system. When National Park Service funding has come up short, Friends of Acadia has been there to lend a helping hand.

There are several ways to help out FOA. You can join the Friends of Acadia (individual membership, $35 per year, family membership, $100 per year) or volunteer your time. FOA organizes volunteer outdoor maintenance programs in the park three times weekly between June and Columbus Day (call the recorded information line for locations, 207-288-3934) and an annual carriage road cleanup day the first Saturday in November. Contact Friends of Acadia for more information (43 Cottage Street, PO Box 45, Bar Harbor, ME 04609; 207-288-3340; www.foacadia.org).

JOHN D. ROCKEFELLER, JR.

Without John D. Rockefeller, Jr.'s deep pockets and even deeper sense of philanthropy, many of Acadia's most popular attractions would not exist. He is the park's most famous benefactor. More importantly, he embodied the true spirit of Acadia.

Rockefeller was born in 1874, the sole male heir to the vast Standard Oil fortune. Influenced by his family's pious values, he was a strict nondrinker and a deeply religious man. He was also a lover of nature, spending as much time as possible outdoors. Although he went to work for Standard Oil after graduating from Brown University, Rockefeller quickly realized that the family business was not for him. In 1910, at the age of 36, he retired from the working world and devoted himself to a life of philanthropy.

Rockefeller first visited Mount Desert Island in college, but it wasn't until he returned in 1908 with his wife, Abbey, that he fell in love with the island. Two years later, Rockefeller bought a spectacular hilltop estate in Seal Harbor. Before long Rockefeller was approached by local philanthropist George Dorr, who was soliciting funds for the creation of a national park. Rockefeller gladly opened his wallet.

In the decades to come, Rockefeller would become Acadia's greatest benefactor, donating one-third of the land in the park. Before Rockefeller came along the park consisted mostly of mountaintops. Rockefeller bought the land in between the mountaintops and donated it to the park. He also spearheaded and financed both the Park Loop Road and the carriage roads—two projects that drew strong opposition at the time. Some conservationists felt the roads would ruin the wild nature of the park. Rockefeller disagreed. A firm believer that nature could make people, "happier, richer, better," Rockefeller argued that roads and paths were necessary to make nature more accessible to the public. Today, few would disagree that Rockefeller's contributions have made the park a better place for all.

How Rich was Rockefeller?

In 1913, shortly before the breakup of Standard Oil, the Rockefeller family fortune was estimated at $900 million—about $15 billion today applying changes in the Consumer Price Index. But when viewed as a percentage of the 1913 Gross National Product, which provides a better measure of the economic clout the Rockefellers wielded at the time, their fortune would have been worth over $200 billion today.

PARK LOOP ROAD

THE PARK LOOP ROAD is Acadia's star attraction. Twisting 27 miles through the spectacular eastern half of Mount Desert Island, it cruises through forests, dips through valleys, skirts the ocean, and rambles past lakes and ponds. After passing by Acadia's most popular sites—Sand Beach, Thunder Hole, Jordan Pond House, Bubble Rock—it climbs to the top of Cadillac Mountain, the island's highest peak. The Park Loop Road is the main artery of the park, pumping millions of visitors through Acadia each year. But no matter how crowded it gets (and during peak season it can get *very* crowded), the Park Loop Road is always worth it. If you only have one afternoon to spend in the park, spend it on the Park Loop Road.

There are three popular ways to explore the Park Loop Road: drive your own car, pay for a guided bus tour, or take the free Island Explorer Shuttle. All have advantages and disadvantages. Taking your own car offers the most flexibility, but traffic and parking can be a hassle during peak season. Guided tours (p.219) offer on-the-spot commentary and remove the hassle of driving and parking, but they whisk you through the park on a set schedule with little time to explore on your own. The Island Explorer (p.19) offers flexibility (shuttle stops at popular destinations about every 30 minutes) and relaxation (no driving, no parking), but it doesn't follow the Park Loop Road in a continuous loop (it's broken up into two routes) and it doesn't go to the top of Cadillac Mountain. Whatever method you choose, plan on spending at least three hours exploring the Park Loop Road. If you do drive your own car, the best place to start is the Hulls Cove Visitor Center, located north of Bar Harbor just off Route 3.

Now, a bit of history. The Park Loop Road was the brainchild of John D. Rockefeller, Jr., who realized the enormous potential a motor road through the park could have. Despite strong opposition from some summer residents who thought the road would ruin the park, Rockefeller spearheaded construction in 1922. The way Rockefeller saw it, automobiles were inevitable. The park could either plan for their arrival carefully or ignore the issue until it was too late. To ensure that the Park Loop Road blended in peacefully with the natural scenery, Rockefeller commissioned renowned landscape architect Frederick Law Olmstead, Jr. to handle the design. Completed in 1953, the Park Loop Road remains one of the most stunning drives in America.

1 Hulls Cove Visitor Center
mile 0

This is Acadia National Park's main visitor center. Inside you'll find a help desk, free park publications (including the indispensable *Beaver Log*, listing seasonal schedules and ranger programs), a giant map of the island, restrooms, and a store overflowing with books, calendars, and other assorted goodies. A small auditorium also shows a free 15-minute movie about the park. The visitor center is open mid-April through October, 8am-4:30pm (8am to 6pm in July and August). During peak summer months, up to 9,000 people pass through the visitor center each day. It's busiest between 10am and 2pm—try to arrive earlier or later if you can.

—— RULES OF THE PARK LOOP ROAD ——

- The speed limit never exceeds 35 mph and is strictly enforced.

- Parking is allowed on the right-hand side of the road between mile 3 and mile 19 (the one-way section of the loop).

- You'll need a park pass (p.104) to access the Park Loop Road. Passes can be purchased at the Hulls Cove Visitor Center, Park Headquarters, Bar Harbor Village Green, Sand Beach entrance station (mile 8.1), Blackwoods Campground, or Seawall Campground.

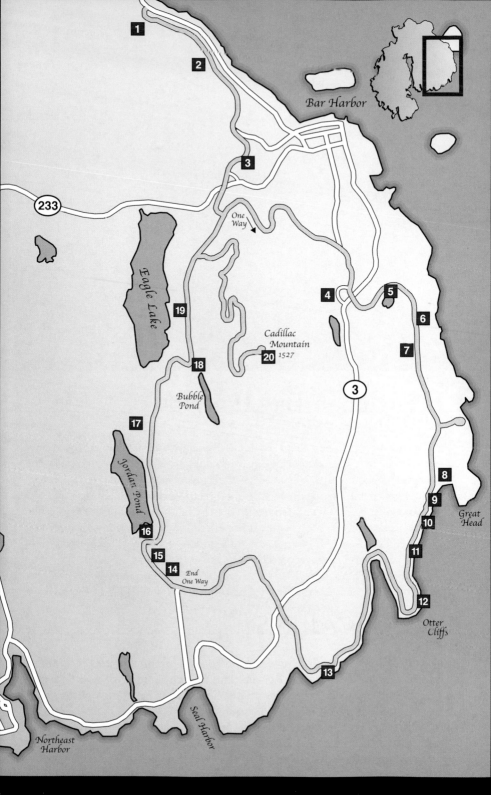

Bar Harbor

233

Eagle Lake

One Way

Cadillac Mountain 1527

3

Bubble Pond

Jordan Pond

Great Head

End One Way

Otter Cliffs

Seal Harbor

Northeast Harbor

2 Frenchman Bay Overlook
mile 0.4

The first stop on the Park Loop Road overlooks Frenchman Bay, bounded by Mount Desert Island to the west and Schoodic Peninsula to the east. From this overlook you can see several of the Porcupine Islands, named for their resemblance to porcupines (arched profiles, pointy pine trees). During the French and Indian War, French gunboats often hid behind the Porcupine Islands to ambush British vessels, and it was from these skirmishes that Frenchman Bay probably got its name. Even after the war, the islands continued to make fabulous hiding places. One of the islands, Rum Key, got its name during Prohibition when rum runners smuggled liquor into Frenchman Bay from Canada.

Today, some of the Porcupine Islands are owned or partially owned by Acadia National Park. Strangely, the islands not owned by the park do not belong to the town of

RAGIN' CAJUNS

In colonial times, the French referred to the coastal region that now includes Canada and parts of Maine as *L'Acadie*, and French settlers in Nova Scotia and New Brunswick were called "Acadians." Following England's victory in the French and Indian War, some of these settlers relocated to Louisiana, where *Acadians* was shortened and drawled to "Cajuns."

Frenchman Bay from Cadillac Mtn.

Bar Harbor (they belong to the town of Gouldsboro, across the bay). The closest island to the overlook is Bar Island, connected to Bar Harbor by a shallow sandbar exposed at low tide. Twice a day, you can walk to Bar Island from Bar Harbor (p.213). In the late 1800s, when Bar Harbor was one of the most exclusive resorts in the world, a courtship developed between a Turkish ambassador and a young lady from Philadelphia. Desperate to win the young lady's heart, the ambassador organized an evening party on Bar Island. Paper lanterns were hung from the trees, violinists played hidden in the woods, and the guests were treated to an underwater fireworks display.

3 1947 Fire Overlook
mile 2.2

In 1947 a massive fire burned over 17,000 acres on Mount Desert Island. Before the fire, the island was covered in an evergreen forest of spruce and fir. Following the fire, sun-loving hardwoods such as maple, beech, and oak flourished in the open spaces. But as the hardwoods grew and shaded the forest floor, shade-loving evergreens once again took root. Someday, the evergreens will reclaim their lost territory. Until then, a mixed forest covers the island. From the 1947 Fire Overlook you can trace the path of the fire, marked by the light green patches of hardwood leaves against dark green evergreens. This contrast becomes surreal in the fall, when the hardwoods' brilliant orange and red foliage seems to reenact the historic blaze.

Coastal Fog

Fog is a fact of life in Downeast Maine, which typically sees 55 or more foggy days each year. Fog is essentially a low-lying cloud that forms when moist air cools to the dew point. Along the coast there are two types of fog: radiation fog and advection fog. Radiation fog forms when the sun goes down and cold ocean water chills the air. It's light and thin and generally burns off by late morning. Advection fog forms far offshore and is blown in by the winds (advected). This is the classic pea-soup fog, and it can linger for days or weeks. Advection fog forms when warm, moist air from the Gulf Stream comes into contact with cold water in the Gulf of Maine. As one Maine sea captain put it in the late 1800s, "You'll find fogs all the world over, but the Gulf Stream fog beats 'em all. It will heave in sooner, stay longer, and become thicker, and go away quicker than any fog I ever met in my voyaging."

Early Maine sailors were highly superstitious of fog. One coastal legend claimed that each time a thick fog descended a phantom ship would appear, with a death to follow...

Porcupine Islands

— legend of ——
The Porcupine Islands

According to an Indian legend, a giant once lived on top of Cadillac Mountain who kept five porcupines as pets. Although he specifically instructed the porcupines never to stray from the mountaintop, one day while the giant was away the porcupines chased one another to the island's shore. When the giant returned and found the porcupines missing, he grew angry. He called out to the porcupines, but they ignored his calls. Furious, the giant began hurling boulders from the mountaintop. (One of those boulders, Balance Rock, can be seen on the Bar Harbor Shore Path today.) Terrified, the porcupines fled into the harbor to escape. As luck would have it, a wandering fairy happened upon the porcupines and turned them into stone, forever protecting them from the giant's wrath.

Sieur de Monts Spring, early 1900s

National Park Service

4 Sieur de Monts Spring
mile 5.6

This mellow oasis is home to the indoor Acadia Nature Center (displays on plants and animals), the tiny Abbe Museum (native history, $2.00 admission), and the Wild Gardens of Acadia (filled with over 300 species of native plants, open dawn to dusk). There's also a covered spring that was once used by Indians and early settlers. The spring is named for French explorer Pierre de Gua, Sieur de Monts ("Sir Mountain"), who was Samuel Champlain's boss when Champlain named Mount Desert Island in 1604. The land here was donated by George Dorr, who built the arched dome over the spring and had "Sweet Waters of Acadia" inscribed on a nearby rock. The inscription was inspired by Dorr's travels in Turkey, where he had seen springs labeled "Sweet Waters of Europe" and "Sweet Waters of Asia." Due to its wet, wooded location, Sieur de Monts Spring is an excellent spot for bird watching. Over 70 bird species have been identified here.

5 Beaver Dam Pond
mile 6.2

This small pond was created by a beaver dam. Beavers are most active at night, but they can sometimes be spotted here at dawn or dusk. By 1900 trappers had exterminated beavers from Mount Desert Island, but in 1920 they were successfully reintroduced to the park. The buildings across the Park Loop Road belong to the Jackson Lab, a private research facility not affiliated with the park.

Sieur de Monts Spring

Beaver Pond

6 Egg Rock Overlook
mile 6.6

This overlook, marked by an obvious pull-off on the left side of the road, provides sweeping views of Frenchman Bay. Egg Rock is the tiny, lighthouse-capped island about two miles offshore—a favorite haunt of harbor seals, who spend their days basking and lounging on the island's rocks. Beyond Egg Rock lies Schoodic Peninsula, the only part of Acadia National Park connected to the mainland.

Egg Rock was named by early coastal settlers who gathered the eggs of seabirds there (a practice now banned to protect the birds). In 1875 a lighthouse was built on Egg Rock to help ships navigate the rocky entrance to Frenchman Bay. Because Egg Rock is so small, the lighthouse beacon was built on top of the keeper's residence to conserve space. (Most lighthouses place their beacon in a separate tower). For over a century, Egg Rock was faithfully manned by lighthouse keepers who lived year-round on the island. The beacon was originally lit by whale oil, which was stored in barrels in the adjacent shack. Whale oil was later replaced by kerosene, which was then replaced by electricity from gas-powered generators. Today, the lighthouse is fully automated, and electricity is delivered from Bar Harbor via an underwater cable. There are also several solar panels propped up to the right of the shack that provide backup energy.

As guardian of Frenchman Bay, Egg Rock has seen some remarkable comings and goings over the years. During World War II a 250-foot German submarine snuck past Egg Rock and deposited two spies at Hancock Point, just north of Mount Desert Island. The spies, carrying $60,000 cash and a bag of diamonds, made their way to New York City before they were captured—an event that made national headlines.

Highseas

Highseas is the spectacular brick building to the right of the Egg Rock overlook. This 32-room mansion was built in 1912 by Princeton professor Rudolf Brunnow. It was intended as a wedding gift for his fiancé, who was then living in Europe. Tragically, she booked her passage to America on the Titanic and perished in the North Atlantic.

In 1924 Highseas was purchased by wealthy New York City divorcée Mrs. Eva Van Cortland Hawkes. The sum: $25,000. Mrs. Hawkes kept a large staff at Highseas that included a butler, two footmen, a downstairs maid, upstairs maid, kitchen maid, personal maid, cook, laundress, cleaning woman, chauffeur, and gardener. During World War II, Mrs. Hawkes threw lavish parties at Highseas for the American and British navies that called to port in Bar Harbor. Champagne flowed freely and lobster Newburg was cooked in 30-gallon drums.

When the great fire of 1947 swept through this part of the island, Highseas was spared destruction by a faithful gardener who kept the mansion doused with water. Following Mrs. Hawkes' death, the estate was donated to the Jackson Lab. Today the building is used as a dormitory for high school and college students working for Jackson Lab.

7 Champlain Mountain
mile 7.3

As you continue past the Egg Rock overlook, you'll flank the eastern face of Champlain Mountain, which rises nearly a thousand vertical feet above the Park Loop Road. The eastern face of Champlain Mountain contains the steepest cliffs on the island, and the famous Precipice Trail (p.172) heads straight up them. The steep cliffs also provide excellent habitat for nesting peregrine falcons (p.64). Peregrines faced extinction in the 1960s for a variety of reasons including hunting, a reduction in prey, and the effects of the pesticide DDT. By 1969 they had completely disappeared from Acadia. In 1984 peregrines were reintroduced to the park as part of a captive breeding program, and since 1991 they have nested on Champlain's steep cliffs. In the spring and early summer, the Precipice Trail is often closed to protect nesting peregrine falcons. During closures, the park sets up viewing scopes in the parking area at the base of the mountain from 9am to noon.

DDT: Savior & Scourge

The insecticide DDT is one of the most fascinating (and controversial) chemicals of the 20th century. Following its introduction in World War II, DDT saved millions of lives by stopping the spread of insect-carried diseases and substantially boosting crop yields. Agricultural corporations hailed it as a modern miracle—a powerful insecticide that posed no risk to humans. In 1948 Paul Muller, the scientist who introduced DDT to the world, was awarded the Nobel Prize.

Then, in 1962, Maine biologist Rachel Carson wrote *Silent Spring*, in which she detailed how DDT was lingering in the environment and killing birds, including peregrine falcons. The book produced an uproar and helped launch the modern environmental movement. Soon, reports began surfacing that DDT also caused cancer in humans, and environmentalists lambasted the pesticide as a modern scourge. In 1972, under intense public pressure, the U.S. government banned DDT and essentially forced many developing countries to do the same.

The ban on DDT has since been heralded as a triumph of environmentalism. But while extensive studies have shown that DDT is almost undoubtedly responsible for killing birds, they have also shown that it poses virtually zero risk to humans—the early claims of cancer in humans turned out to be completely false. And in some developing countries, the ban has had horrific, rarely reported consequences. Nothing has proven as effective as DDT for controlling insect populations in the developing world, and it has been estimated that between 30 and 50 million people, mostly children, have died of insect-carried diseases that could have been prevented through the use of DDT.

The ban on DDT is a complex issue with no easy answers. It did demonstrate, however, that both agricultural corporations and environmentalists were quick to rush to judgement in the name of virtue—with little regard to unintended consequences.

Peregrine falcon chicks

8 Sand Beach
mile 8.7

Sheltered in a secluded cove just off the Park Loop Road, Sand Beach is one of the most beautiful places in Maine. On clear summer days, hundreds of visitors flock here to soak in the scenery and sunshine. If the water wasn't so bone-chillingly, teeth-chatteringly cold, Sand Beach would be perfect. But this is Maine, and even in the summer ocean temperatures rarely crack 60 degrees. Whether you find a swim here refreshing or masochistic, you can rest assured the beach will be packed on sunny days in July and August. During this time, finding a parking spot in one of the two adjacent lots is like winning the lottery (yet another reason to ride the Island Explorer shuttle. Two popular hikes, the Beehive (p.170) and the Great Head Trail (p.178) lie within walking distance of Sand Beach.

So why on earth—or rather, on the infamously rock-bound coast of Maine—did a sandy beach form here? The shape of the cove shelters Sand Beach from powerful waves and currents, which allows sand to gather. But the "sand" is actually a combination of sand and the crushed shells of sea creatures such as urchins, mussels, and barnacles. A close examination of the beach particles reveals blues, greens, purples, and creams. A smattering of crushed granite adds some pink and white. In the winter, storms often pull large amounts of sand away from the beach, sometimes revealing the hull of an old ship that crashed in 1911 on Old Soaker (the rock ledge at the head of the cove) and washed up on the beach. Back then, Sand Beach was owned by J.P. Morgan. His granddaughter donated the beach to the park in 1949.

Sand Beach was featured in the 1999 movie *The Cider House Rules.*

Sand Beach

9 The Ocean Trail

Stroll along the Ocean Trail and bask in the park's most spectacular stretch of shoreline. The landscape between Sand Beach and Otter Cliffs is classic Acadia—rugged, rocky, and resplendent. And the easy (essentially flat) Ocean Trail takes you past it all. Crashing waves? Salty breeze? Scented pines? Done, done, and done. If ever there was a reason to stop and explore the Park Loop Road on foot, the Ocean Trail is it.

The Ocean Trail parallels the Park Loop Road for about two miles from Sand Beach to Otter Cliffs, passing Thunder Hole and Monument Cove along the way. The trail starts at the far end of the upper parking lot at Sand Beach and runs next to the Park Loop Road all the way to Thunder Hole. Past Thunder Hole the trail veers away from the road, offering a bit more seclusion. If you're riding the Island Explorer, you can make a one-way trip of the Ocean Trail by catching a shuttle at either Thunder Hole or Otter Cliffs.

Now a stern warning: If you choose to step off of the path and onto the rocks, be extremely careful—especially in high seas. The ocean is powerful, dangerous, and unforgiving. This isn't Seaworld. It's nature. And nature isn't looking out for your safety. Every so often a careless visitor gets swept off the rocks by a wave. The result is often lethal, with waves pounding the helpless victim against the jagged shore. It's graphic, I know, but it happens. Use caution.

National Park Service

10 Thunder Hole
mile 9.4

Thunder Hole is the most overhyped attraction in the park. During stormy seas when waves rush into this rocky chasm, it produces a thundering boom and mountains of spray. But the vast majority of the time Thunder Hole does little more than gurgle and slosh. If you're lucky, it might let out a weak burp. Booming or not, hundreds of tourists flock to Thunder Hole each day in the summer, hoping for a bit of magic. You can thank whoever came up with the name "Thunder Hole" for that. If it were named "Sloshing Hole" or "Hole That Thunders Only Occasionally," most people would just keep driving. But with its mysteriously macho moniker, this otherwise unexceptional crack has become one of Acadia's must-see destinations.

That being said, you can still get a sense of Thunder Hole's stormy showmanship even in smaller seas. The trick is to visit at just the right time. Arrive two hours before high tide and you might—*might*—catch some excitement. But don't get your hopes up. If you do happen to visit Acadia during a storm, however, head directly to Thunder Hole and get ready for some action.

So why does Thunder Hole thunder? A small cave at the end of the chasm is responsible for the booming sound. When powerful waves rush in, air is trapped and compressed in the cave. Ultimately, when the pressure becomes too great, air roars out of the cave with a thundering *BOOM!* During particularly large storms, the boom can sometimes be heard for miles.

"Visitors to Mount Desert but half understand or appreciate its wonders if they do not visit the cliffs in a storm."
—Oliver B. Bunce, Picturesque America, 1872

Monument Cove

11 Monument Cove
mile 9.7

Most people drive past Monument Cove without even realizing it's there. But this tiny cove, sheltered by tall pine trees on either side, is a testament to the power of erosion. The "monument" of the cove is the obelisk-like spire at the north end. Over thousands of years, erosion widened natural cracks in the rock walls surrounding the cove, and as chunks of the rock fell away, the monument was left behind. The fallen chunks were then tumbled by the waves, eroding to form rounded, pumpkin-sized boulders. Like Sand Beach, Monument Cove is partially sheltered from waves and currents. But here, where the cove is much more exposed to the ocean, waves and currents are powerful enough to wash away any sand or small cobblestones that might form, leaving the heavy boulders behind.

12 Otter Cliffs
mile 10.1

These vertical cliffs rise 110 feet above the ocean, making them irresistible to rock climbers who scamper up Otter Cliffs all summer long. Just beyond the cliffs is a shallow ledge in the water marked by a bell buoy. Historians believe the explorer Samuel Champlain smashed his boat into this ledge when he first sailed to Mount Desert Island—a collision that required repairs in nearby Otter Cove. Despite Otter Cliff's name, there are no sea otters here. In fact, there are no sea otters on the entire East Coast. Otter Cliffs and Otter Cove—as well as Otter Point and Otter Creek—were probably named after river otters (which *are* found in Acadia) or the now-extinct sea mink, which was sometimes mistaken for an otter.

13 Little Hunters Beach

A small wooden staircase leads down to this peaceful, cobblestone beach. The cobblestones here are notable because they formed from rocks in Acadia's "Shatter Zone." Roughly 420 million years ago, a large plume of magma rose up under Mount Desert Island's previously formed bedrock and cooled into granite. But when the scorching hot magma came into contact with the cool bedrock above, it caused the bedrock to shatter into pieces. Some of those pieces fell into the magma, and when the magma cooled the pieces were suspended in the granite like plums in plum pudding. These "plum pudding" rocks make up the Shatter Zone. At Little Hunters Beach you can often see chunks of the older, mostly darker bedrock (the "plums") in the granite cobblestones. The rusty coloration on some rocks comes from iron oxide. In the 1800s cobblestones from Maine beaches like this one were used to pave the streets of Boston, New York, and Philadelphia. Note: It is now illegal to remove cobblestones from Acadia National Park.

Otter Cliffs

Little Hunters Beach

Jordan Pond Gatehouse

14 Wildwood Stables
mile 15.3

Located at the end of a right turnoff on the Park Loop Road, Wildwood Stables offers one- and two-hour horse-drawn carriage rides along Acadia's famous Carriage Roads. Trips go to Day Mountain (sweeping views of the coast), Cobblestone Bridge (an exquisite stone bridge), or the Jordan Pond House (p.138). Private carriage rides are also available, and stables can be rented for private horses. (Open mid-June to mid-Oct, 207-276-3622, www.acadia.net/wildwood)

15 Jordan Pond Gatehouse
mile 16.3

John D. Rockefeller, Jr. had this gatehouse built in 1932 as a checkpoint to keep automobiles off the Carriage Roads. (Today it serves as a residence for lucky park personnel.) Rockefeller felt the architecture in many national parks was haphazard, and he was determined to make Acadia's buildings better. In 1929 he sent architect Grosvenor Atterbury on a tour of national parks to study their architectural successes and faults. Atterbury returned with several guidelines for successful national park architecture, most importantly: (1) Buildings shouldn't compete with the local scenery, and (2) if no local style of architecture exists for reference, a suitable foreign style should be chosen. Because no local style existed in Acadia, Atterbury designed the Jordan Pond Gatehouse based on a French Romanesque design. He also set the building at the edge of the road where, surrounded by forest, it wouldn't compete with the scenery.

Wildwood Stables

16 Jordan Pond House

mile 16.4

For over a century, visitors have come here to feast on the food and the scenery. Lunch and dinner are served, but many people sit down simply to savor the house specialty: popovers served with strawberry jam. Nobody—not even those who are already full, not even those on a diet—should miss out on popovers. Part pastry, part balloon, oven-fresh popovers would be mouth-watering in any corner of the world. But munched on the lawn in front of Jordan Pond ... well, let's just say that most things this good aren't legal. (Open mid-May to mid-October. In the summer, the last Island Explorer shuttle leaves the Jordan Pond House for Bar Harbor at 8:50pm)

The original Jordan Pond House opened its doors in 1896. Back then, it was little more than a rambling farmhouse. John D. Rockefeller, Jr. bought the rambling farmhouse in the 1920s and later donated it to the park. In 1979 a fire destroyed the original Jordan Pond House. The present building was constructed in 1982.

At 150 feet, Jordan Pond is the deepest body of freshwater on the island. At the north end of Jordan Pond lie the Bubbles, two scrumptiously symmetrical (from this angle, at least), glacially carved mountains. (North Bubble, on the left, is actually taller than South Bubble, but it's farther away so it looks like it's the same height.) You can walk to the base of the Bubbles along the Jordan Pond Trail, a moderate 3.2-mile hike that loops around the perimeter of Jordan Pond. A popular local joke claims the Bubbles earned their name when an early explorer set eyes on the mountains and was immediately reminded of his girlfriend: "Bubbles."

Jordan Pond House, early 1900s

The Bubbles

Rock climber, South Bubble

Bubble Rock

17 Bubble Rock
mile 18

As the Park Loop Road rises above the eastern shore of Jordan Pond, it heads between the Bubbles (on your left) and Pemetic Mountain (on your right). Keep your eyes out for rock climbers on the cliffs of South Bubble, then shift your gaze upward for a glimpse of Bubble Rock. Perched precariously on a high ledge, Bubble Rock is a glacial erratic, deposited during the last Ice Age when glaciers carried it here from a spot 20 miles away. When the glaciers melted, Bubble Rock settled on the ledge. Although the 14-ton boulder looks like it could topple over at any moment, it's actually quite secure. You can see for yourself via the short Bubble Rock Trail (rating: moderate, 0.7 miles round-trip, starts from the Bubble Rock parking area).

18 Bubble Pond
mile 19

A small parking lot on the right marks the pull-off for this pristine pond. Nestled between Cadillac and Pemetic Mountains, Bubble Pond is your best bet for peace and tranquility along the Park Loop Road. A carriage road traces the western shore (great for a quick stroll), but swimming is prohibited here (public water supply).

19 Eagle Lake Overlook
mile 20.1

Past Bubble Pond the Park Loop Road rises above the western shore of Eagle Lake, the island's second largest body of freshwater. A pull-off on the left provides sweeping views of the gorgeous scenery.

20 Cadillac Mountain
mile 23.6

Saving the best for last, the Park Loop Road turns right at mile 23 and climbs to the top of Cadillac Mountain. At 1,527 feet, Cadillac is the highest mountain on the island and the highest point on the Atlantic north of Rio de Janeiro. The road to the summit is filled with hairpin turns and sweeping 360-degree views.

Several pull-offs along the road provide spectacular views of the island. At mile 21.7 you can check out the western side of the island (Eagle Lake, Sargent Mountain, Pemetic Mountain), and several pull-offs between mile 21 and 22.5 let you soak in the views to the east (Bar Harbor, Porcupine Islands, Frenchman Bay). A small pull-off at mile 23.3 reveals the island's southern shore and the many smaller islands beyond (Cranberry Isles, Swans Island, Isle au Haut). Mile 23.4 marks the turn-off to the Blue Hill Overlook, the most popular sunset spot on Mount Desert Island (arrive well before sunset during peak season to snag a space in the tiny parking area).

Contrary to popular belief, Cadillac's summit does not lie above treeline. But conditions here are so harrowing that only small, rugged plants can survive. Plants living on the summit of Cadillac (and the summits of several other mountains) must cope with strong winds, freezing temperatures, and rapid erosion from run-off. The constant erosion and sparse vegetation lead to poor soil development, which prevents larger plants (such as trees) from taking root. (Note: Each year millions of visitors explore Cadillac's summit. All those footsteps add up, so the park recommends sticking to Cadillac's half-mile loop trail to preserve the sparse vegetation. If you do go off the trail, walk only on exposed granite.)

Between October 7 and March 7, Cadillac Mountain is the first place in the United States to see the sunrise.

In the late 1800s a small cog railroad chugged up the side of Cadillac (then called Green Mountain). The half-hour ride cost $2.50 and brought visitors to the summit where they could spend the night in the 50-room Summit Hotel. The railroad was short-lived, however, going bankrupt after only a decade. The hotel was torn down in 1896.

Cadillac Mountain

SCHOODIC PENINSULA

S CHOODIC PENINSULA IS a rugged finger of land jutting into the Atlantic just east of Mount Desert Island. It forms the eastern boundary of Frenchman Bay, and its 2,000 acres form the only part of Acadia National Park connected to the mainland. Lying in the shadow of Mount Desert Island, Schoodic has few bragging rights when it comes to scenery. There are no towering mountains, hidden lakes, or sandy beaches here. But Schoodic Peninsula is hardly the black sheep of the park. Its rugged shores offer a rare glimpse of raw, unfiltered, undeveloped coastal Maine. What's more, its relatively remote location keeps it sheltered from the swarms of tourists that descend on Mount Desert Island each summer, giving Schoodic Peninsula a more subtle, peaceful charm. If crowded roads and screaming children are fraying your nerves, Schoodic might be the scenic Valium you need.

Although Schoodic Peninsula lies only five miles east of Mount Desert Island as the seabird flies, it's a little over an hour drive (50 miles) by car. A better option is the Bar Harbor Ferry (207-288-2984, cost: $25 adults, $15 children round-trip), which runs boat shuttles between Bar Harbor and Winter Harbor, a small fishing village near the peninsula. Starting in the summer of 2003, the Island Explorer also began offering a Schoodic route that loops around the peninsula and passes through Winter Harbor. (As of this writing, the service was running on a trial basis; check its present status before you go.)

Schoodic's one-way road makes a full loop around the Peninsula when combined with a short stretch of Route 186. Unlike Mount Desert Island's crowded Park Loop Road, the Schoodic Loop Road is almost always mercifully free of traffic, making it great for hiking. (If you take the Bar Harbor Ferry you can bring your bike along for an extra $5.)

Schoodic Peninsula was added to the park in 1929. Prior to the addition, Acadia National Park was called Lafayette National Park. The original name was chosen in 1919 to reflect America's pro-French sentiment in the wake of World War I. Later, Schoodic was donated by three Anglophile sisters on the condition that the name of the park be changed to something less French. George Dorr, the park's first superintendant, suggested the name Acadia based on an early name for the region. Apparently unknown to the sisters, "Acadia" was based on *L'Acadie*, a name given by—*sacre blu!*—the French.

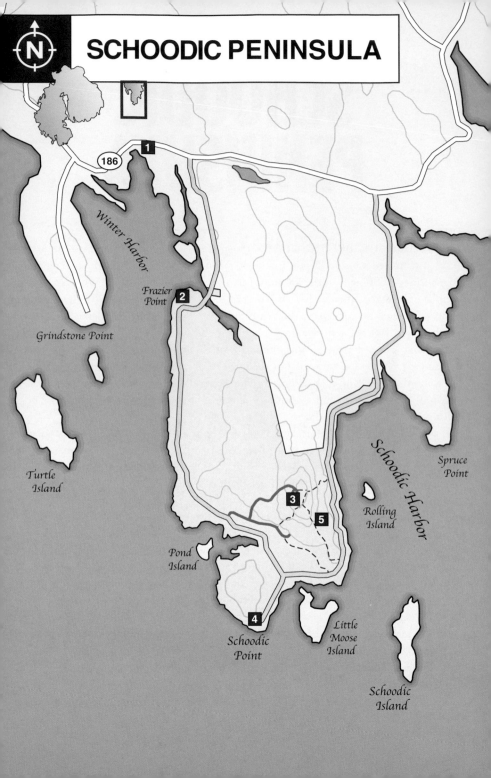

N

186

Winter Harbor

Grindstone Point

Frazier
Point

2

1

Turtle
Island

Pond
Island

3

5

Rolling
Island

Schoodic Harbor

Spruce
Point

4

Schoodic
Point

Little
Moose
Island

Schoodic
Island

1 Winter Harbor

This tiny coastal village (pop. 1,000) is located about two miles east of the entrance to Schoodic Peninsula. It's home to fishermen, whose boats fill the harbor, and the super rich, whose summer houses line the shores of Grindstone Neck. In addition to picturesque scenery, Winter Harbor boasts two worthy restaurants: The Fisherman's Inn (7 Newman Street, 207-963-5585) and Mama's Boy Bistro (10 Main Street, 207-963-2365). There's also the nine-hole Grindstone Neck Golf Course (207-963-7760). And every second Saturday in August, Winter Harbor hosts an annual lobster festival, featuring live music, lobster boat races, lobster, lobster, and lobster. For more on Winter Harbor and other nearby towns check out www.acadia-schoodic.org.

2 Frazier Point Picnic Area

Located just past the Mosquito Harbor Bridge, Frazier Point offers million dollar views at picnic basket prices. The picnic area includes tables, fire rings, drinking water, and outhouses. If you brought a car and a bike, you can park your car here and bike the rest of the Schoodic Loop Road. Past Frazier Point Picnic Area, Schoodic Loop Road becomes one-way, but you can loop back to Frazier Point via Route 186.

NOTE: Parking is not permitted in the right lane of Schoodic Loop Road. There are, however, a handful of pull-outs where you can park your car, allowing you to explore some overgrown trails that lead to the rugged cliffs on Schoodic's western shore.

3 | Schoodic Head

Located at the end of a short side road, Schoodic Head is the highest point on Schoodic Peninsula (440 feet). Although it's views are somewhat obscured, it still makes a fun side trip. About 2.5 miles past the Frazier Point Picnic Area, an unpaved road turns left off the main road and continues for about a mile to a small parking area. From the parking area a short access road leads to Schoodic Head.

4 | Schoodic Point

Continuing on the main road, you'll pass a former U.S. Navy base which now houses the Schoodic Education and Research Center. A two-way road then turns right to Schoodic Point. Situated at the tip of the peninsula, Schoodic Point offers sweeping views of the Atlantic. Unlike Mount Desert Island, which is sheltered from high seas by several smaller offshore islands, Schoodic Peninsula is exposed to the full force of the open Atlantic, making waves particularly powerful here. Use caution.

5 | Anvil Trail

The Anvil Trail rises to a promontory 180 feet above sea level, then continues on to Schoodic Head. The trail starts across the street from the Blueberry Hill parking area. From the trailhead it's roughly one mile to Schoodic Head.

Town Landing

ISLE AU HAUT

L OCATED 15 MILES southwest of Mount Desert Island by sea, Isle au Haut is Acadia's most far-flung parcel of property. While Mount Desert Island is defined by tourism, Isle au Haut is a genuine working Maine island where fishing has been the primary occupation for over 200 years. Today, about 80 people live year-round on Isle au Haut, and roughly half of the island's 5,800 acres belong to Acadia National Park—representing arguably the most pristine coastal landscape in Maine. If "rugged," "remote," and "rock-bound" are some of your favorite words, it's time to add "Isle au Haut" to your vocabulary.

Isle au Haut ("High Island") was named by French explorer Samuel Champlain in 1604. Although Champlain traveled up and down the coast of Maine on his voyage of discovery, he named very few places along the way. But Isle au Haut, with its tall mountains rising hundreds of feet above the water, was simply too obvious a landmark to remain anonymous. Not surprisingly, the island's high elevation makes it great for hiking; over 18 miles of rugged trails crisscross the park. But other than hiking, relaxing, and soaking in the scenery, there's not much else to do on Isle au Haut—which is exactly why people love it.

Now the hard part: getting to Isle au Haut, which reaches farther into the Atlantic (15 miles) than any other large island in Maine. The first step is to drive to Deer Isle, an island six miles north of Isle au Haut that's connected to the mainland by a bridge. At the southern tip of Deer Isle is the town of Stonington (a two-hour drive from Bar Harbor) where you can catch the mailboat/passenger ferry to Isle au Haut. Cost: about $35 per person round-trip (first-come, first-served). Schedules vary depending on the season. From mid-June to early September (except Sundays) the ferry also stops at Duck Harbor, located near the southern tip of the island. Contact the Isle au Haut Boat Company for current schedules and fares (207-367-5193, www.isleauhaut.com).

Day tripping to Isle au Haut (catching the morning and evening ferry) gives you about seven hours on the island. But it takes enough effort to get here that you might as well spend the night, giving you plenty of time to explore the island. There are two lodging options on Isle au Haut: cozy, expensive inns near the town landing, or rugged, inexpensive lean-to shelters at the park's Duck Harbor Campground. Both require advance reservations (see following pages for details).

Isle au Haut's southern shore

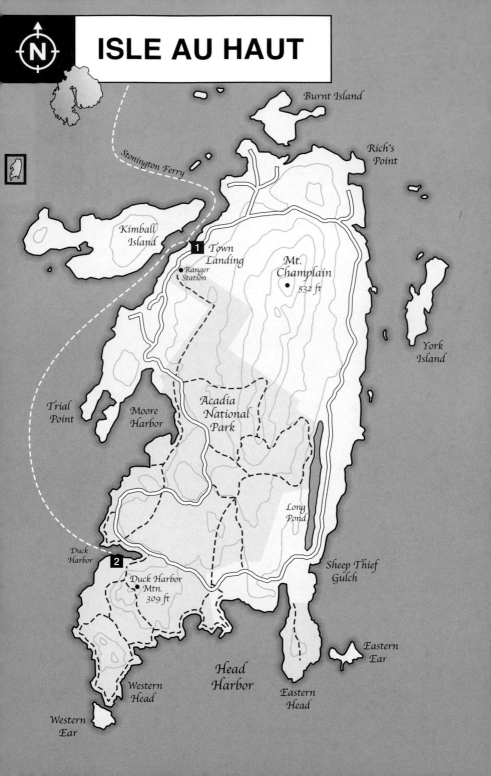

The Keeper's House

1 Isle au Haut Town Landing

Isle au Haut's small town landing is the island's social hub. Just up the road is a small general store that offers the only food for sale on the island (mostly snacks). Just down the road is Acadia National Park's Isle au Haut ranger station (207-335-5551).

At its peak in the 1880s, Isle au Haut was home to over 350 people, mostly fishermen who benefitted from the island's remote location. When gas-powered engines arrived in the early 1900s, fishermen could commute from the mainland, and since then Isle au Haut's population has fallen dramatically. Among the current locals: Linda Greenlaw, best-selling author of *The Hungry Ocean* and *The Lobster Chronicles*, and who was chronicled herself in *The Perfect Storm*.

Lodging

The Keeper's House—The only lighthouse with rooms to rent in Maine, and one of the most eco-friendly inns in New England. Offers candlelight dinners with exceptional gourmet meals. ($310–385 per night, two-night minimum July through Labor Day, often booked months in advance; 207-469-1174, www.thekeepershouse.com)

The Inn at Isle au Haut—Located on the less-visited eastern side of Isle au Haut, offering views of Mount Desert Island. Simple and elegant. ($250–315, two-night minimum on weekends; 207-335-5141, www.innatisleauhaut.com)

Bel's Inn—Located next to the town landing. Cozy and convenient. ($250–265 peak, $150–165 off-peak; 207-335-2201)

Duck Harbor Mountain

Duck Harbor Campground

2 Duck Harbor Campground

The five lean-to shelters at Duck Harbor Campground (operated by Acadia National Park) offer the only camping on Isle au Haut. Each 8-foot by 12-foot lean-to sleeps up to six people, and facilities include a fire ring, picnic table, pit toilet, and water pump. (The water pump is located 1,600 feet from the campground—bring a container to haul water). Pets are not allowed, and all trash must be packed out. The campground is open from May 15 to October 15. Reservations are required prior to arrival. Contact the park for a reservation request form (207-288-3338, www.nps.gov/acad), and return the completed form with a check for $25 anytime after April 1. (Be aware that dates in July and August are highly competitive; include alternate dates.) One reservation covers camping for up to six people, with a maximum stay of five nights May 15–June 15, three nights June 15–September 15, and five nights September 15–October 15. Note: From Mon–Sat during peak season (late June to early September) the mailboat ferry stops at the landing in Duck Harbor, about a quarter mile from the campsite. Off season you'll have to hike five miles from the town landing to reach Duck Harbor Campground.

Hiking Isle au Haut

Isle au Haut's best hiking trails are concentrated at the southern tip of the island, not far from Duck Harbor Campground. Among the most popular: Duck Harbor Mountain, which rises 300 feet above Duck Harbor, and the Cliff Trail, which bobs in and out of dark spruce forests and skirts the rocky shore. Although the trails on Isle au Haut are often rugged and overgrown, they're always worth it.

Hiking south of Duck Harbor

Gorham Mountain

HIKING

I F HIKING IS your fancy, Acadia will tickle it until you cry (hopefully in a good way). Over 130 miles of hiking trails crisscross the island, forming an interconnected web of ambulatory elegance. Even if Acadia's trails consisted of nothing more than crumbling dirt paths, they'd be incredible. But here on Mount Desert Island, home to influential (i.e. rich and charitable) summer residents, the trails have been spruced up beyond belief. Many feature handcrafted stone steps that gracefully lead you past otherwise challenging terrain. In 1999 Friends of Acadia established a $15 million endowment to keep Acadia's trails in peak condition forever. This is rich man's hiking, folks—free of charge. I have never, in all my travels, found coastal hikes as consistently elegant and stunning as those found in Acadia. If you visit Mount Desert Island without going on at least one hike, you should return to the mainland ashamed.

All hikes in Acadia are day hikes; overnight backpacking is not allowed. Hikes range from flat strolls to nearly vertical climbs to everything else in between. No matter what your level of physical fitness, there's a hike in Acadia for you. The only hard part is picking which hikes to leave out. (It's tough to play favorites, but if I had to pick a Top Three I'd go with The Beehive, The Precipice, and Penobscot Mountain). All trails in Acadia are easy to follow, but keep your eyes out for the blue blazes (paint markings on rocks or trees) and cairns (small piles of rocks) that lead your through potentially confusing sections.

Note: The 11 hikes listed on the following pages are, in my opinion, the best hikes on the island. Hiking these trails will keep you busy for days. But if your thirst for hiking exceeds that of the average visitor, I highly recommend picking up a copy of Tom St. Germain's *A Walk In The Park*. The bible of Acadia hiking, *A Walk In The Park* can take you anywhere on the island you want to go.

TRAIL RATINGS

EASY — Level, sometimes rocky ground that may include minor rises.

MODERATE — Gradual inclines with uneven footing.

STRENUOUS — Steep, rocky, difficult inclines.

LADDER — Strenuous hiking that requires climbing iron rungs or ladders.

Joe Hanlon

THE BEEHIVE

SUMMARY   Short and sweet, The Beehive is one of the most popular trails in Acadia. Rising to the top of a beehive-shaped dome just south of Champlain Mountain, the trail provides unbeatable views of Sand Beach and Great Head Peninsula. Nestled in the sparkling granite near the top of the Beehive is The Bowl, a gem-like mountain pond where you can soak your feet or jump in and go for a swim. Although the Beehive is one of the shorter trails in Acadia, it's not for the faint of heart. A few steep sections require climbing iron rungs, and several precipitous drop-offs won't sit well with anyone with a fear of heights.

TRAILHEAD   The Bowl Trail starts across the Park Loop Road from the upper Sand Beach parking area. Follow the Bowl Trail 0.2 miles to its intersection with the Beehive Trail, which veers off to the right.

TRAIL INFORMATION	THE BEEHIVE
DISTANCE 1.6 miles round-trip	**RATING** Ladder
APPROXIMATE HIKING TIME 1 hour, 15 minutes	
ELEVATION CHANGE 450 feet	

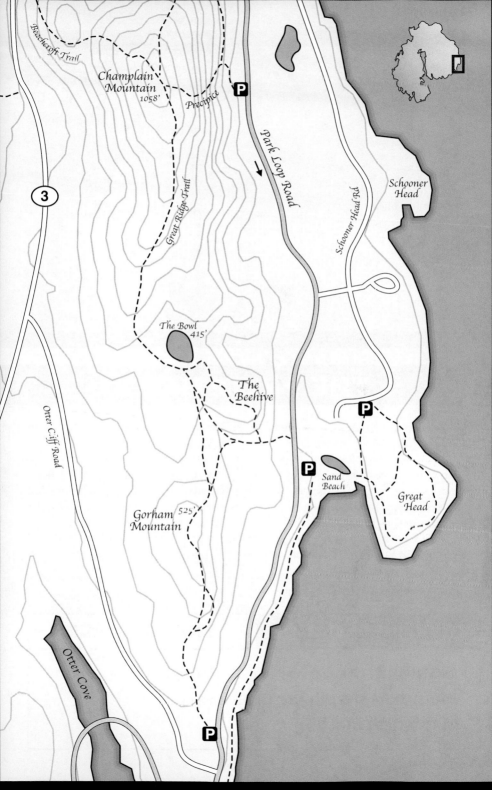

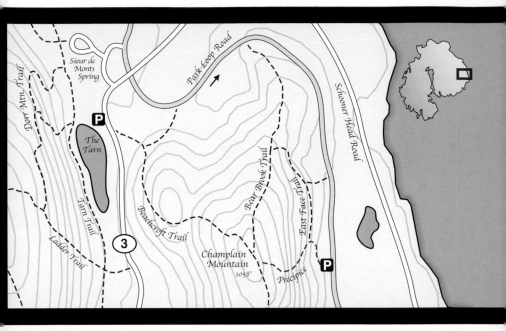

THE PRECIPICE

SUMMARY   Rising nearly 1,000 feet up the dramatic east face of Champlain Mountain, The Precipice is considered by many to be the most challenging trail in the park. It's certainly the most famous. A jungle gym of iron rungs guides hikers up this otherwise unhikable cliff, which is usually closed from April to mid-August to protect nesting peregrine falcons. Despite the hype, it takes more mental strength than physical strength to conquer the Precipice. This ain't Everest—it's a manicured trail, and other than some exposed, 100-foot-plus drop-offs and a few steep sections that require ladder-style climbing, the Precipice is no worse than many other challenging, yet less-heralded hikes in Acadia. But if you do have a fear of heights, stay away.

TRAILHEAD   The Precipice Trial starts from the Precipice parking area on the Park Loop Road, two miles south of the Sieur de Monts entrance off Route 3.

TRAIL INFORMATION	THE PRECIPICE
DISTANCE 1.8 miles round-trip	**RATING** Ladder
APPROXIMATE HIKING TIME 2 hours	
ELEVATION CHANGE 930 feet	

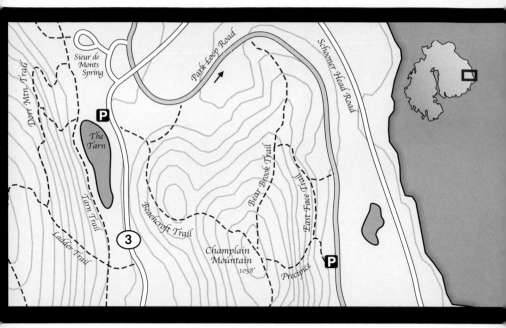

BEACHCROFT PATH

SUMMARY Like the Precipice, the Beachcroft Path rises to the top of Champlain Mountain, which offers the best views of Frenchman Bay on the island. But unlike the cliff-hugging, vertigo-inducing Precipice, the Beachcroft Path rises up the gentler, western side of Champlain, making for a much milder hike. That being said, you're still rising nearly 1,000 vertical feet over a short distance (1.6 miles). But with dozens upon dozens of exquisite stone steps and wide-open views along the way, the Beachcroft Path makes that rise as accommodating as possible.

TRAILHEAD The Beachcroft Path trailhead begins on the east side of Route 3, across from the parking area at the north end of The Tarn (the swampy pond between Champlain Mountain and Dorr Mountain, just south of Bar Harbor).

TRAIL INFORMATION	BEACHCROFT PATH
DISTANCE 3.2 miles round-trip	**RATING** Strenuous
APPROXIMATE HIKING TIME 2 hours	
ELEVATION CHANGE 978 feet	

GORHAM MOUNTAIN

SUMMARY   Gorham Mtn. offers the best views of any moderate hike in the park. Great for families with young children, the trail rises up Gorham Mtn. above the spectacular shoreline between Sand Beach and Otter Cliffs. Cadillac Cliffs, a short and strenuous spur trail along the way, passes an ancient sea cave. (The cave was at sea level 12,000 years ago after the glaciers melted, which sent ocean levels higher. But free of the weight of the glaciers, the land slowly rebounded to its present height.) For an extended hike you can follow the trail past the summit of Gorham Mtn. and follow it down to the Sand Beach parking area. From there you can catch an Island Explorer shuttle or hike the Ocean Trail back to the Gorham Mtn. trailhead.

TRAILHEAD   The Gorham Mtn. Trail starts from the Gorham Mtn. parking area on the right side of the Park Loop Road, about a mile past Thunder Hole.

TRAIL INFORMATION	GORHAM MOUNTAIN
DISTANCE 2 miles round-trip	**RATING** Moderate
APPROXIMATE HIKING TIME 1 hour, 15 minutes	
ELEVATION CHANGE 425 feet	

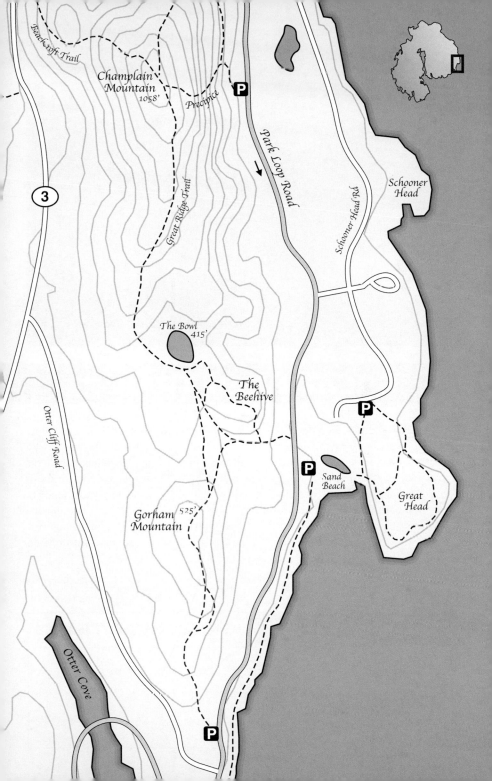

GREAT HEAD TRAIL

SUMMARY This brisk hike rises above the eastern side of Sand Beach to Great Head, a rugged and rocky peninsula that marks one of the easternmost points on the island. Perfect for a little exercise in the middle of a lazy day at the beach, the Great Head Trail sees a lot of action in the summer. At the tip of Great Head, 145 feet above the ocean, lies the crumbling remains of an old tower that belonged to Louisa Saterlee, who was given both Great Head and Sand Beach as a present from her father, legendary financier J.P. Morgan. The tower, which included a tea room, a salon, and an observatory, burned down in the Great Fire of 1947. Shortly thereafter, the land was donated to the park.

TRAILHEAD The Great Head Trail starts at the eastern end of Sand Beach.

TRAIL INFORMATION	GREAT HEAD TRAIL
DISTANCE 1.8 miles round-trip	**RATING** Moderate
APPROXIMATE HIKING TIME 1 hour	
ELEVATION CHANGE 145 feet	

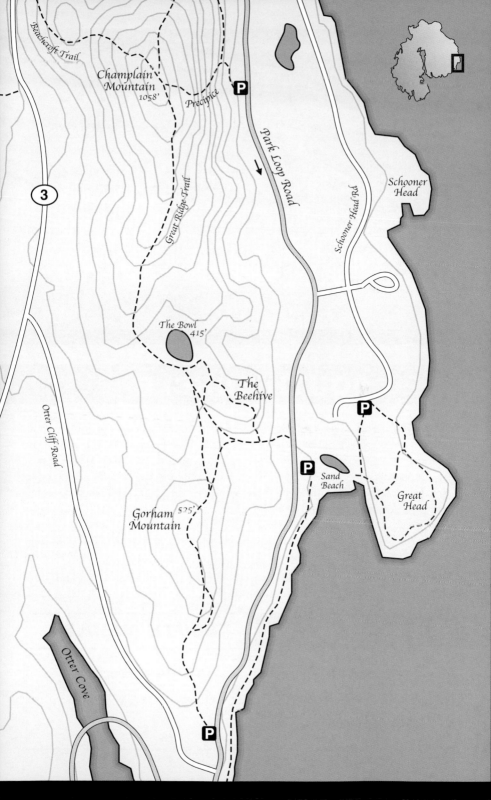

SOUTH BUBBLE

SUMMARY   This short, challenging loop offers sweeping views of Jordan Pond and passes by ever-popular Bubble Rock. From the Bubble Rock parking area the trail dips down to the northern shore of Jordan Pond, then rises up the steep face of South Bubble. The footing up South Bubble is often loose and gravelly—a tenuous scramble not recommended for novice hikers or those with a fear of heights (but highly recommended for those with a taste for adventure and a love of spectacular views). At the top of South Bubble check out Bubble Rock (p.145), then follow the trail north as it heads down to the parking area. Or if you've got some extra time, check out the North Bubble Trail, which offers great views of Eagle Lake.

TRAILHEAD   The South Bubble loop starts from the Bubble Rock parking area, 1.5 miles north of the Jordan Pond House on the Park Loop Road.

TRAIL INFORMATION	SOUTH BUBBLE

DISTANCE 1.6 miles round-trip   **RATING** Strenuous

APPROXIMATE HIKING TIME 1 hour

ELEVATION CHANGE 468 feet

PENOBSCOT MOUNTAIN

SUMMARY   The trail up Penobscot Mountain offers spectacular views of Jordan Pond and the southern shores of Mount Desert Island. Starting near the southern shore of Jordan Pond, the trail rises quickly through dense forest, scrambles up a few iron rungs, and then bursts onto the vista-soaked granite ridge of Penobscot Mountain. After passing over the peak, the trail dips back into the forest and descends rapidly to the northern tip of Jordan Pond. (Just past the start of the descent, a 0.2-mile trail leads to beautiful Sargent Mtn. Pond.) Once at the northern tip of Jordan Pond, you can follow the Jordan Pond Shore Trail back to the trailhead. Note: Fresh popovers at the Jordan Pond House never taste better than following the immediate completion of the Penobscot Mountain Trail.

TRAILHEAD   The Penobscot Mtn. Trail starts behind the Jordan Pond House.

TRAIL INFORMATION	PENOBSCOT MTN.
DISTANCE 6 miles round-trip	**RATING** Strenuous
APPROXIMATE HIKING TIME 3 hours	
ELEVATION CHANGE 900 feet	

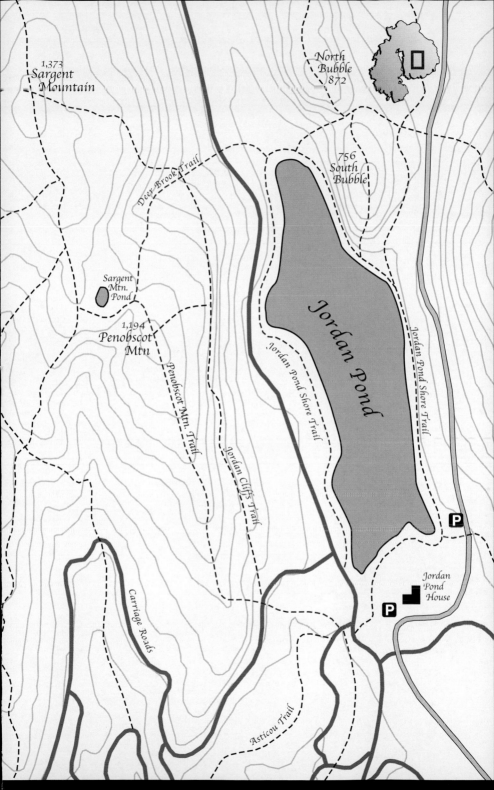

Penobscot Mountain

Joe Hanlon

CADILLAC MTN. WEST FACE

SUMMARY Cadillac Mountain's West Face Trail is the most direct route to the top of the island's highest peak. The lure of hiking (as opposed to driving) Cadillac is irresistible to many people, and with good reason—the views along the way are incredible. Although Cadillac's North Ridge Trail is easier (rating: moderate) and therefore more popular, the views along the West Face Trail are significantly more rewarding. If you're going to spend all that energy hiking up Cadillac, the West Face trail is definitely worth the extra effort (provided you're in good physical shape—be prepared to burn some serious calories climbing the trail's many steep sections).

TRAILHEAD The Cadillac Mountain West Face Trail starts near the Bubble Pond parking area on the Park Loop Road. Walk towards the pond, take a left at the shore, and cross a short plank bridge. The trailhead is on your right.

TRAIL INFORMATION	CADILLAC WEST FACE

DISTANCE 2.8 miles round-trip   **RATING** Strenuous

APPROXIMATE HIKING TIME 4 hours

ELEVATION CHANGE 1,000 feet

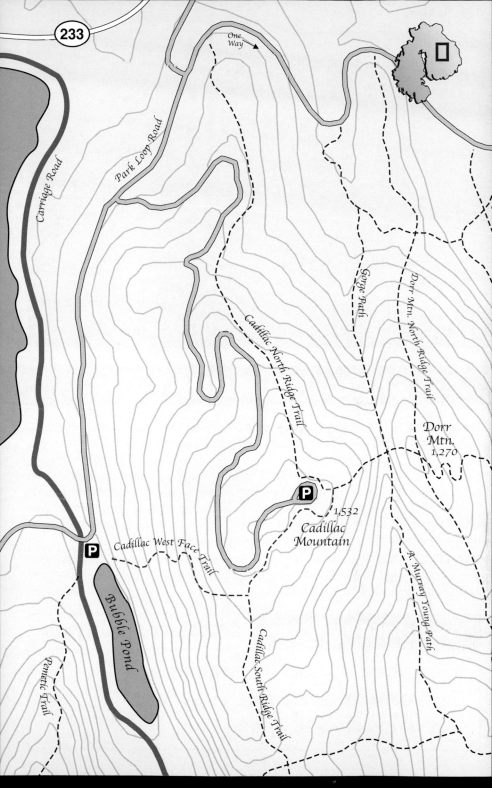

Joe Hanlon

SARGENT MOUNTAIN

SUMMARY   The hike to the top of Sargent Mountain is one of the longest and most rewarding in the park. If Cadillac Mountain is Mount Desert Island's Everest, Sargent Mountain is the island's K2. At 1,373 feet, Sargent is only 154 feet shorter than Cadillac, but it boasts far more impressive views of the island's southern shores. Lying in the middle of a complex web of trails, there are several possible approaches. For my money, the Harbor Brook Trail/Maple Spring Trail loop is the best. After following gurgling Harbor Brook, you'll pass under one of the carriage road's most beautiful stone bridges, then rise through the forest to Sargent's exposed granite peak.

TRAILHEAD   The Hadlock Brook Trail starts across the street from a parking area on the west side of Route 198, just north of Upper Hadlock Pond (about a mile north of the town of Northeast Harbor).

TRAIL INFORMATION	SARGENT MOUNTAIN
DISTANCE 5 miles round-trip	**RATING** Strenuous
APPROXIMATE HIKING TIME 4 hours	
ELEVATION CHANGE 1.150 feet	

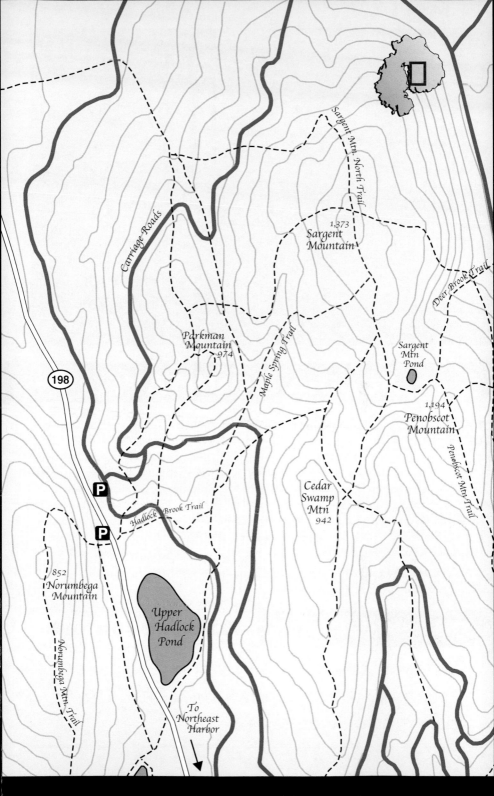

ACADIA MOUNTAIN

SUMMARY   Acadia Mountain is drenched in spectacular views of Somes Sound, the only fjord on the East Coast. Located on the western, "quiet" side of the island, Acadia Mountain flies under the radar of many first-time visitors. But those in the know consider it one of the best hikes on the island. After rising through the forest to a spectacular lookout on top of Acadia Mountain, the trail drops nearly 600 feet in about a half mile. Near the base of the mountain a short side trail leads to Man o' War Brook. This small waterfall, cascading directly into Somes Sound, was used by 18th and 19th century ships (Man o' Wars) to replenish their water supplies. Back on the trail, you'll reach a junction with a wide access road that leads back to the trailhead.

TRAILHEAD   The trail starts across from the Acadia Mtn. parking area on Route 102, just north of Southwest Harbor.

TRAIL INFORMATION	ACADIA MOUNTAIN
DISTANCE 2.6 miles round-trip	**RATING** Strenuous
APPROXIMATE HIKING TIME 1 hour, 30 minutes	
ELEVATION CHANGE 581 feet	

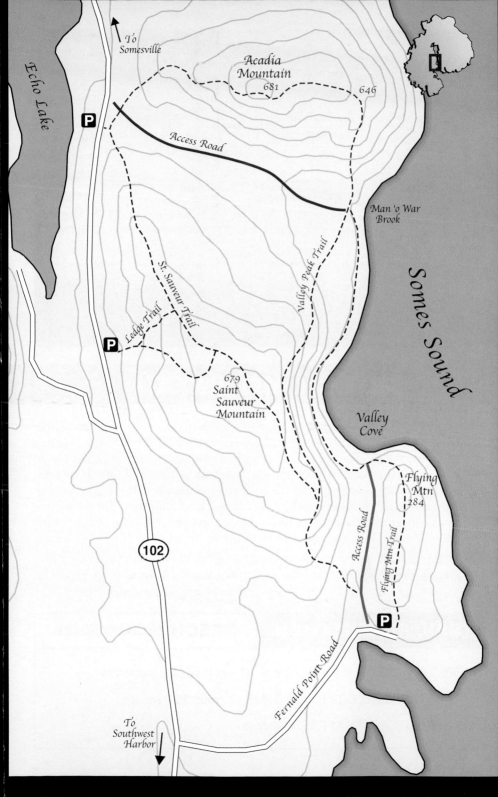

Joe Hanlon

BEECH MOUNTAIN

SUMMARY   This peaceful hike rises to Beech Mountain, revealing some of the island's most overlooked and underrated scenery. From the Beech Mountain parking area, follow the Valley Trail through a lush forest, then rise up a series of exquisite granite steps toward Beech Mountain's peak. The fire tower on top of Beech Mountain was last used in 1976 (today, most fire patrols are done by small planes). The tower is closed to the public except for special weekends in the fall. From the summit follow the western branch of the Beech Mountain Trail loop (which provides sweeping views of Long Pond) back to the parking area.

TRAILHEAD   Follow Route 102 south of Somesville and turn right onto Pretty Marsh Road. Turn left onto Beech Hill Road, which dead ends at the Beech Mountain parking area. The Valley Trail starts at the south end of the parking area.

TRAIL INFORMATION	BEECH MOUNTAIN

DISTANCE 2.9 miles round-trip   **RATING** Moderate

APPROXIMATE HIKING TIME 1 hour, 30 minutes

ELEVATION CHANGE 589 feet

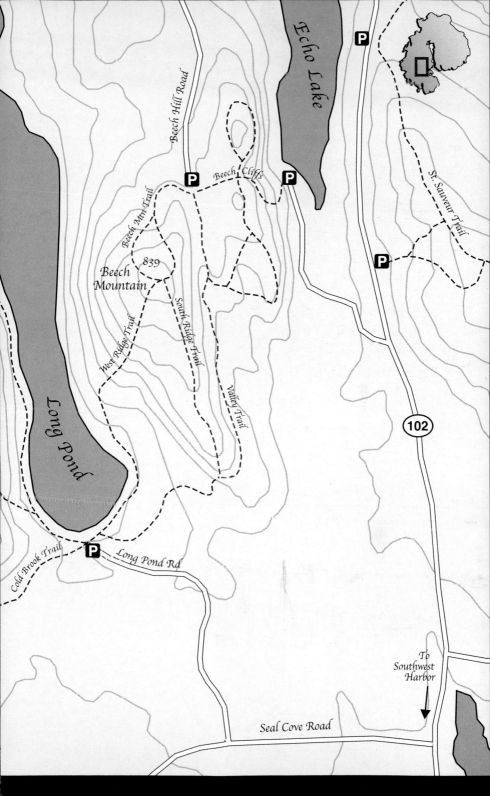

CARRIAGE ROADS

ACADIA'S CARRIAGE ROADS are like a fairy tale come to life. Originally constructed on the private estate of John D. Rockefeller, Jr., most were later donated to the park for the enjoyment of the public. Today, over 57 miles of pristine broken-stone roads twist through Acadia, revealing the island's otherwise hidden, lush interior—a land of leafy forests, sparkling streams, and stunning lakes. Sprinkled along the carriage roads are 17 exquisite stone bridges, hand-crafted by stonemasons out of native rock. When the bridges first opened, they regularly saw the comings and goings of horse-drawn carriages. But bicycles have long since become the most popular mode of transportation on the carriage roads. Today, many people consider a peddle-powered romp along the carriage roads to be the highlight of their trip to Acadia.

The carriage roads form a web-like network of car-free roads on the eastern half of Mount Desert Island. They extend from Paradise Hill (not far from downtown Bar Harbor) south to the Rockefeller family estate (still privately owned but open to the public) in Seal Harbor. There is no official start or end to the carriage roads. There are, however, six popular parking areas next to the carriage roads where most people begin their journey. From there you can choose your own adventure. Although the intricate network of roads can be confusing at first, numbered signposts at every intersection, used with the maps on the following pages, make it hard to get lost. Bicycles can be rented in Bar Harbor (p.219), or you can head to Wildwood Stables near Seal Harbor to pay for a genuine, old-fashioned horse-drawn carriage ride (p.136). Hiking the carriage roads is another option. Note: Twelve miles of carriage roads in Seal Harbor are open only to hikers and horseback riders—no bicycles. Keep your eyes out for "No Bicycle" signs posted at intersections.

HISTORY OF THE CARRIAGE ROADS

The fascinating story of the carriage roads traces its roots to the year 1837, when a wooden bridge first connected Mount Desert Island to the mainland. For decades this minor improvement produced relatively little change in island life; back then ships were still the primary mode of transportation. But with the dawn of the automobile age in the late 1800s, that tiny bridge suddenly became a vital link between Mount Desert Island and the modern world—a fact that did not sit well with many summer residents who came to Mount Desert Island specifically to *escape* the modern world.

By the time Henry Ford introduced his Model T to the masses in 1908, automobiles were already banned on Mount Desert Island. The ban served two purposes: it allowed summer visitors to take refuge from the sputtering, soot-spewing automobiles that were flourishing in big cities; and it allowed year-round residents to limit the pretentious lifestyles of those rich enough to actually afford automobiles. All that changed with the Model T. As moderately priced automobiles flooded the nation, local islanders were determined not to be left out of the fun. In 1909 a group of locals lobbied to repeal the ban on cars. Their efforts were blocked by a group of wealthy summer residents who fought hard to keep the ban in place. Two years later a temporary compromise was reached limiting cars to the town of Bar Harbor. But the locals kept at it, and by 1915 cars were allowed in every town on Mount Desert Island.

Among the summer residents most alarmed at this turn of events was John D. Rockefeller, Jr., who had recently purchased a home in Seal Harbor as a summer refuge from New York City. At a time when most wealthy Manhattan businessmen commuted to work in shiny new cars, Rockefeller drove himself to work in a horse-drawn carriage—a habit that spoke volumes about his poor fit among the office buildings of New York. Happiest outdoors, Rockefeller coped with the stress of Manhattan office life by chopping wood after work. After a few years at the helm at Standard Oil, Rockefeller abandoned his post and devoted himself to a life of philanthropy.

When Rockefeller arrived in Seal Harbor in 1910, the Great Automobile War—as it was later dubbed—was just beginning. Perhaps sensing the inevitable, Rockefeller began building a series of broken-stone roads on his sprawling Seal Harbor estate where he could enjoy the simple pleasures of a horse-drawn carriage ride, free from cars. As his network of roads grew, he decided to connect them in a continuous loop. But to do so required passing through land owned by the Hancock County Trustees of Public Reser-

For out they turned, the summer folk, and when the count they wrote,
They'd kept the autos out of town by an enormous vote,
So glory hallelujah, hip, hip, and three times three;
Mount Desert Town, of fair renown, from autos will be free.

—Herber Weir Scythe, 1913

vations, the founding fathers of Acadia National Park. Rockefeller tried to buy the land in question, but his offer was refused. He was allowed, however, to build roads through the land with the knowledge that they might one day be shut down.

Rockefeller accepted this risk, and over the next decade he continued to expand his network of roads through the park. Things went well until a proposed road near Northeast Harbor drew heat from local conservationists, who felt the road would be a blight on the natural landscape. Northeast Harbor summer resident George Wharton Pepper fired off a letter to Rockefeller. "In my judgement," he wrote, "it would be a serious mistake to extend your well conceived system of roads into this area." Rockefeller reluctantly bowed

Rockefeller's carriage roads were opposed by summer residents who felt they would ruin the park.

to the opposition and halted construction of the road in question.

By this point, many people were already using and enjoying Rockefeller's roads, and most were highly supportive of his plans. A group of locals circulated a petition urging Rockefeller to continue his road construction, and the *Bar Harbor Times* published an op-ed piece in full support of the carriage roads. But despite the outpouring of support, the ever cautious Rockefeller stayed out of the fray and did not resume construction of the road in question.

The sudden controversy was particularly worrisome to George Dorr, the savvy and spirited superintendant of the park. Dorr knew that Rockefeller's deep pockets could make a world of difference for the young park and did not want to alienate him. Recognizing Rockefeller's obvious enthusiasm for road building, Dorr suggested that Rockefeller help build a gravel "access" road north of Jordan Pond. Rockefeller jumped at the idea. Soon, the park's "access" road had expanded to include a series of gravel roads connected to Rockefeller's previously constructed carriage roads. Although on paper the new roads were ordered by Dorr, it was Rockefeller who studied and planned them, simply making "suggestions" as to where they might be placed.

Rockefeller financed these new roads with the condition that a new motor road also be constructed through the park. Although Rockefeller was hardly thrilled with the steady stream of automobiles pouring onto the island, he realized they were inevitable, and he wanted to plan for them wisely.

Rockefeller's proposed motor road immediately drew heat from the same small group of wealthy summer residents that had opposed his carriage roads. Again it was George Pepper, by this time a Senator from Pennsylvania, who led the charge. Pepper contacted Secretary of the Interior Hubert Work and used his influence to halt construction of both the motor road and the new carriage roads. Pepper and others felt the new park was already drawing too many people to Mount Desert Island. A motor road, they argued, would only encourage more to come. Such feelings were summed up in a 1924 article in the *Boston Evening Transcript*: "Protests were especially emphatic from the view-point of many of the summer residents, who had long enjoyed the blissful quiet and primitive beauty of the island. They freely stated their fear that the proposed development would bring in a 'peanut crowd' of the Coney Island type, and that the park would speedily be littered with egg shells, banana peels, old tin cans."

Rockefeller saw things differently. As he had pointed out during a similar road building incident at another national park, "What are these parks for ...? The average American can't afford to go into the secluded areas or to have private trips into the parks. He must travel on such a highway. That's the whole point of the national park system." Rockefeller, ever the populist, believed in opening the parks to the common man, as well as to those who required easy access such as the elderly and the handicapped.

Rockefeller had the full support of year-round residents, who welcomed the flood of money that road construction and increased tourism would bring. With the backing of local residents and Maine politicians, Rockefeller and Dorr pushed hard to continue construction of both the motor road and the carriage roads. In the face of such strong opposition, Senator Pepper backed down. Shortly thereafter, the Secretary of the Interior came to the island to examine the situation firsthand. After viewing the roads, he concluded that they were indeed a worthy improvement. He granted his full blessing for the roads already underway, with the stipulation that all future roads be approved by his office.

Emboldened by the overwhelming public support for his cause, Rockefeller charged ahead with plans for an even larger network of carriage roads and an expanded motor road. To bypass the approval demanded by Secretary Work, Rockefeller built new roads on land earmarked but not yet donated to the park. Only when the roads were finished would the land be transferred to the park. Another round of protests erupted, but this time there was nothing that could be legally done to halt the construction.

By 1940 Rockefeller's grand vision was complete. A 57-mile network of broken stone roads stretched from Bar Harbor to Seal Harbor, passing mountains, lakes, and ponds along the way. Curving gracefully through the woods, the roads revealed some of the park's most beautiful, hidden scenery. Every twist and turn was personally selected by Rockefeller, whose knowledge of road building and hands-on involvement in the undertaking were legendary. Rockefeller also commissioned 17 exquisite stone bridges along the carriage roads. Each bridge, unique in design, was handcrafted by stonemasons and financed by Rockefeller at extraordinary cost.

When all was said and done, Rockefeller had spent nearly 30 years and several million dollars building the carriage roads. When construction began in 1913, horse-drawn carriage rides were still a popular element of island life. By 1940, however, they had turned into a quaint pastime for rich. At the same time, bicycle use had taken off in America. Rockefeller was aware of this fact, and he was one of the first to encourage opening the carriage roads to bicycles. Today, bicycles are the most popular way to explore the carriage roads.

Following Rockefeller's death in 1960, the carriage roads started to fall into disrepair. To remedy the situation, Friends of Acadia established a multimillion dollar endowment for the ongoing upkeep of the carriage roads. After several years of rehabilitation, Mr. Rockefeller's roads were restored to their full glory, and they are now as magnificent as ever.

"When I thought a thing was worth doing, I made up my mind that the annoyances, the obstacles, the embarrassments had to be borne because the ultimate goal was worthwhile."

—John D. Rockefeller, Jr.

ISLAND TOWNS

ff

Bar Harbor

BAR HARBOR

FILLED WITH MORE shops, restaurants, and hotels than all other towns on the island combined, Bar Harbor is the unofficial capital of Mount Desert Island. Its narrow streets and ramshackle buildings, perched on a hill overlooking the shore, make it the quintessential Maine Coastal Town. Ice cream shops, trinket stores, and the smell of fresh seafood round out the effect. To some it's a tourist trap. To others it's a vibrant slice of Downeast Maine. No matter what your take, chances are you'll end up in Bar Harbor at some point on your trip.

The heart of Bar Harbor is the T-intersection of Main Street and Cottage Street, located about two blocks up from the town pier. Both streets are sardine-packed with shops and restaurants that offer a true study in contrasts: upscale galleries sell pricey artwork near novelty stores selling plastic lobsters; gourmet restaurants compete with greasy spoons; a Christmas store is located steps away from a biker shop selling bowie knives and ninja stars. It's hard to put your finger on the retail pulse of Bar Harbor, which means there's something for everyone here.

Equally incongruous is the social fabric of Bar Harbor, which is more like a patch work quilt. Fannypacked retirees, ragged hippies, Gore-tex clad outdoor buffs, casual fleece yuppies—all find fertile ground in Bar Harbor. There are also plenty of hard working locals, college party kids, and seasonal workers from Eastern Europe who have flocked to the island in recent years to earn American dollars worth a fortune back home.

Although famous for its shops and restaurants, Bar Harbor is also the jumping off point for many of the island's most popular outdoor adventures—sea kayaking, whale watching, sailing cruises, etc. When rain puts the lid on outdoor fun, Bar Harbor's two movie theaters and multiple museums will keep you—and the rest of the island—entertained for hours.

During peak season in July and August, Bar Harbor is flooded with visitors—*especially* when cruise ships are in town. Each year about 80 cruise ships call to port in Bar Harbor, dropping anchor among the Porcupine Islands. (Some are so big that they actually *look* like one of the Porcupine Islands.) As the cruise ships disgorge hundreds of passengers onto the town's already busy streets, long lines often form at popular shops and restaurants. If you happen to visit Bar Harbor when one (or two) enormous ships are in port, consider heading elsewhere and exploring Bar Harbor another day.

BAR HARBOR

N

Town Pier

Bar Island

Bar Island Hike

Shore Path

Grant Park

Wayman Lane

Livingston Rd.

1

Main St

Newport

The Field

Stephens Ln

Albert Meadow

Derby Lane

Atlantic Ave

Hancock St

14

3

9

4

Village Green

12

13

5

6

Rodick

Kennebec

10

School St

West St

Cottage St

High St

7

Ledgelawn Ave

Bridge St

Roberts Ave

Greeley Ave

Glen Mary Rd

Mt Desert St

Spring St

2

11

3

Ash Place

Holland Ave

Kebo St

233

3

College
of the Atlantic

8

WALKING BAR HARBOR

1 BAR HARBOR SHORE PATH

This easy stroll wraps around the eastern tip of Bar Harbor, passing by multimillion-dollar mansions and offering fantastic views of Frenchman Bay and the Porcupine Islands. (Note: Parts of the Shore Path pass over private property. Be respectful.) To get to the Shore Path, walk toward the town pier and then follow the path that passes in front of the Bar Harbor Inn. The inn started out as the Reading Room Clubhouse, a private, all-male "literary club" founded in 1887 where "most of the reading was done through the bottom of a cocktail glass." Farther down the Shore Path is Balance Rock, a large precariously balanced boulder that was carried here by glaciers during the last Ice Age. When the glaciers melted, Balance Rock settled into its unlikely position. Near the end of the Shore Path, you'll see the Bar Harbor breakwater, a man-made stone wall that shelters Bar Harbor from large offshore waves. Local lore claims the breakwater was financed by J.P Morgan so large waves wouldn't spill cocktails on his yacht when he visited Bar Harbor.

2 BAR ISLAND

Twice a day when the tide goes out, an underwater sandbar connects Bar Harbor to Bar Island. At low tide you can stroll across the exposed sandbar to Bar Island and follow a short path to an overlook filled with stunning views of Bar Harbor. The sandbar starts at the end of Bridge Street, about a half mile west of the town pier. Check the local papers for tide schedules. There's about a three-hour window (90 minutes before and after low tide) when you can walk across the sand bar. (Note: Parts of Bar Island are private property. Be respectful.)

Bar Harbor from Bar Island

Bar Harbor Shore Path

WALKING BAR HARBOR (continued)

HISTORICAL WALKING TOUR

For $12 per person, a costumed guide will lead you through Bar Harbor, dishing out facts and gossip about the rich and famous who vacationed here in the late 1800s. Great for history buffs. Tickets available at Acadia Bike and Canoe (48 Cottage Street, 207-288-9605).

VISITOR INFORMATION

3 BAR HARBOR CHAMBER OF COMMERCE

The friendly staff here offers a wealth of Bar Harbor information. Great for locating last-minute lodging. Open daily 8am–5pm summer, 8am–4:30pm weekdays off-season (93 Cottage Street, 207-288-5103, www.barharborinfo.com).

4 VILLAGE GREEN

You can ask questions, purchase park passes, and pick up free park publications at this tiny buildings located on the north side of the Village Green.

MUSEUMS

5 ABBE MUSEUM

This large, well-funded museum is devoted to native culture in Maine. Tools, crafts, and other cultural artifacts are on display. The Abbe Museum also offers workshops and children's programs. A small gift shop sells books and traditional crafts. Summer hours: 9am–5pm Sun–Weds, 9am–9pm Thurs–Sat. Spring & Fall hours: 9am–5pm. Admission: $6 adults, $2 children (26 Mount Desert Street, 207-288-3519, www.abbemuseum.org).

6 BAR HARBOR WHALE MUSEUM *recommended*

This tiny museum has great displays on whales and other sea life found in the Gulf of Maine. Its star attraction is a full skeleton of a minke whale. Free admission. Open daily June to October, 10am–8pm (52 West Street).

7 BAR HARBOR HISTORICAL SOCIETY

The best place to learn about Bar Harbor's opulent Cottage Era. Old photos of lost mansions and fashionable visitors are the real draw here, but the Historical Society also offers a wealth of information regarding all things Bar Harbor. Open late June to mid-October, Monday–Saturday, 1pm–4pm. Free admission (33 Ledgelawn Ave., 207-288-0000, www.barharborhistorical.org).

MUSEUMS (continued)

8 GEORGE B. DORR NATURAL HISTORY MUSEUM

Located on the campus of the College of the Atlantic (0.5 miles north of downtown Bar Harbor on Route 3), this small museum is devoted to the natural history of Mount Desert Island. The museum features exhibits on local animals and a touch tank filled with crabs, starfish, sea cucumbers, and other intertidal creatures. The museum also organizes Family Nature Camp, six one-week programs offered between late June and mid-August ($625 per adult, $250 per child; includes food and lodging, reservations essential). The museum is open mid-June to Labor Day, 10am–5pm. Admission: $3.50 adults, $1 children (105 Eden Street, Route 3, 207-288-5395, www.coamuseum.org).

BAR HARBOR OCEANARIUM

Located 8.5 miles northwest of Bar Harbor on Route 3, the Bar Harbor Oceanarium is a bit out of the way, but great for families—especially on a rainy day. The Oceanarium features live harbor seals, a touch tank, a salt marsh walk, and a working lobster hatchery where thousands of baby lobsters are nurtured from birth to be released into Maine waters. If you want to learn more about lobsters, this is the place to start. Open Mon–Sat, 9am–5pm, mid-May to late October. Admission: $10 adults, $6 children (Route 3, 207-288-5005, www.theoceanarium.com).

BOAT TRIPS

FRIENDSHIP V – WHALES/PUFFINS *recommended*

This triple-decker, 112-foot, 200-passenger, jet-powered catamaran cruises at speeds up to 40 mph. Trips last 2–3 hours and travel about 25 miles south of Mount Desert Island where whales (humpback, minke, finback) are most commonly spotted. Puffin cruises head out to Petit Manan Island, the southernmost limit of the Atlantic puffin's breeding range. Price: $45 adults, $25 children, $8 children under six (1 West Street, Town Pier, 207-288-9800, www.barharborwhales.com).

BAY KING III – WHALES *recommended*

The newest member of the Bar Harbor Whale Watch Company's fleet—a high-speed, twin-hull luxury catamaran, built in 2001. The *Bay King III* offers nearly identical whale watching trips as the *Friendship V*, with slightly cheaper rates for adults. (1 West Street, Town Pier, 207-288-9800, www.barharborwhales.com).

MISS SAMANTHA – LOBSTERS/SEALS

The single-deck *Miss Samantha* features an onboard touch tank filled with starfish, sea urchins, and sea cucumbers. Trips last 1.5 hours, during which time lobster traps are hauled up and seals are viewed up close. Price: $20 adults, $15 children, $5 children under 6 (1 West Street, Town Pier, 207-288-9800, www.barharborwhales.com).

BOAT TRIPS (continued)

THE ACADIAN – NATURE CRUISE

This medium-sized, double-decker boat offers narrated two-hour nature cruises of Frenchman Bay. Weather permitting, *The Acadian* cruises down the eastern shore of Mount Desert Island (prime habitat for bald eagles and multimillion-dollar mansions), swings over to Egg Rock (lighthouse, harbor seals), then motors through the gorgeous Porcupine Islands. Porpoises and seabirds are commonly spotted along the way. Price: $25 adults, $15 children, $5 children under six (1 West Street, Town Pier, 207-288-9800, www.barharborwhales.com).

LULU – LOBSTERS/SEALS *recommended*

The *Lulu* offers two-hour trips on a traditional Maine lobster boat. The limit of 12 passengers offers a highly personal experience. As Captain John motors around Frenchman Bay, he hauls up lobster traps and points out fascinating facts about lobsters, seals, and local history. Price: $25 adults, $15 children (55 West Street, Harborside Dock, 207-963-2341, www.lululobsterboat.com).

SEAL – UNDERSEA LIFE *recommended*

The *Seal's* 2.5-hour "Dive-in-Theater" cruise features an underwater diver who captures live video footage of the ocean floor that's projected back onboard. The diver then surfaces with a number of sea creatures—starfish, hermit crabs, etc.—for visitors to see and touch. Extremely popular with children. Price: $30 adults, $20 children (27 Main Street, 207-288-3483, www.divered.com).

MARGARET TODD – SAILING CRUISE

This gorgeous 151-foot vessel is the first four-masted schooner to sail Maine waters in over half a century. It offers two-hour cruises around Frenchman Bay, three times daily. A sunset cruise features live music. Price: $30 adults, $20 children (Bar Harbor Inn Pier, 207-288-4585, www.downeastwindjammer.com).

RACHEL B. JACKSON – SAILING CRUISE

A 67-foot working replica of an 1890s coastal schooner, offering two-hour trips in Frenchman Bay. Passengers are allowed to get hands-on with the crew, helping to steer and raise the sails. Sails four times daily (including a sunset cruise). Also available for private trips, including "boat & breakfast" overnights. (123 Eden Street, 207-288-2216, www.rachelbjackson.com).

BAR HARBOR FERRY – PASSENGER SERVICE

Offers daily passenger service between Bar Harbor and Winter Harbor. This is a great way to get to Schoodic Peninsula (p.153). Price (round-trip): $25 adults, $15 children, $5 bike (207-288-2984).

SEA KAYAKING

COASTAL KAYAKING TOURS

The oldest, most experienced kayak tour operator on the island. Guided day trips range from $35 to $70. Multiday trips feature island camping or overnight stays at coastal inns. (48 Cottage Street, 800-562-8615, www.acadiafun.com).

NATIONAL PARK SEA KAYAK TOURS

Offers guided day trips and multiday camping trips. Day trips: $45 per person. Operates Memorial Day to late September (39 Cottage Street, 800-347-0940, www.acadiakayak.com).

AQUATERRA ADVENTURES

Offers guided day trips and an overnight trip to Winter Harbor. Day trips: $30 to $50 (1 West Street, 207-288-0007, www.aquaterra-adventures.com).

BIKE RENTALS

ACADIA BIKE & CANOE

Rates: $20 per day (small discount with advance reservation), $15 half-day (48 Cottage Street, 800-526-8615, www.acadiabike.com).

BAR HARBOR BICYCLE SHOP

Rates: $20 per day, $15 half-day (141 Cottage Street, 207-288-3886, www.barharborbike.com).

BUS TOURS

ACADIA NATIONAL PARK TOURS

Offers a 2.5-hour naturalist-narrated bus tour of Bar Harbor and Acadia National Park. Trips depart downtown Bar Harbor at 10am and 2pm, May–October. Price: $20 adults, $10 children (tickets available at Testa's Restaurant, 53 Main Street, 207-288-0300, www.acadiatours.com).

OLI'S TROLLEY

In July and August, Oli's offers a one-hour trolley/bus ride that passes by historic mansions and heads to the top of Cadillac Mountain. The tour departs five times daily between 10am and 6pm. They also offer a 2.5-hour Acadia National Park tour departing at 10am and 2pm, May–October. Price: $20 adults, $10 children (58 Cottage Street, 207-288-9899, www.acadiaislandtours.com).

OUTDOOR GEAR

CADILLAC MOUNTAIN SPORTS

The largest selection of outdoor gear on the island—hiking boots, rain gear, rock climbing gear, maps, books, you name it. Open year-round (26 Cottage Street, 207-288-4532, www.cadillacsports.com).

CINEMA

9 CRITERION THEATRE

This historic Art Deco theater shows Hollywood blockbusters and hosts concerts and other events (35 Cottage Street, 207-288-3441, www.criteriontheatre.com).

10 REEL PIZZA

Quality independent films on two screens. Their concession stand sells popcorn and fresh pizza (33 Kennebec Street, 207-288-3811).

BOOKS

SHERMAN'S BOOKSTORE

Extensive selection of popular books, including a comprehensive local section. Also sells gifts, stationary, and a good mix of out-of-town newspapers (56 Main Street, 207-288-3161, www.shermans.com).

GROCERIES

11 DON'S SHOP'N SAVE

The largest grocery store on the island (86 Cottage Street, 207-288-5680).

12 J.H. BUTTERFIELD

Gourmet food and fine wine (152 Main Street, 207-288-3386).

13 THE ALTERNATIVE

Specializes in organic food (16 Mount Desert Street, 207-288-8225).

14 BAR HARBOR FARMER'S MARKET

Small vendors sell fresh vegetables, locally made cheeses, and other assorted goodies. Located in the YMCA parking lot on Main Street just south of downtown Bar Harbor. Open 10am–2pm every Sunday, mid-May to late October.

CONCERTS & FESTIVALS

FOURTH OF JULY

Bar Harbor's busiest day. Festivities include a blueberry pancake breakfast, seafood festival, parade, live music, and fireworks at night. Check local papers for details.

BAR HARBOR TOWN BAND

Free concerts at the Bar Harbor Village Green. Showtime: 8pm every Monday and Thursday in July and August.

ARCADY MUSIC FESTIVAL

High quality, classical concerts at various locations in July and August (207-288-2141, www.arcady.org).

BAR HARBOR MUSIC FESTIVAL

Weekend concerts featuring classical, jazz, and pop (207-288-5744)

MOUNT DESERT GARDEN CLUB TOUR

Every other year, members of the Mount Desert Garden Club showcase their private gardens on the second or third Saturday in July. Contact the Bar Harbor Chamber of Commerce for further details.

RESTAURANTS

There are dozens of restaurants in Bar Harbor. Listed below are my personal favorites. Bar Harbor restaurants are pretty consistent when it comes to price, with most offering entrees in the $10–$20 range. Pricier and cheaper restaurants are noted.

BURNING TREE

Fantastic seafood. This upscale, low-key restaurant is a bit off the beaten path, but cherished by those in the know. Located about five miles south of downtown Bar Harbor. Open for dinner only (Route 3, 207-288-9331).

15 CAFE BLUEFISH

Quaint and classy. An understated, gourmet restaurant tucked away on Cottage Street. Famous for their lobster strudel—one of the tastiest meals on the island. (122 Cottage Street, 207-288-3696).

16 CAFE THIS WAY

Delicious, well-crafted food in a relaxed, friendly atmosphere. Serves up hearty breakfasts and dinners. One of the best breakfasts in Bar Harbor (14 Mount Desert Street, 207-288-4483).

RESTAURANTS (continued)

17 EDEN

Gourmet organic vegetarian cuisine with vegan options. The meals here are hearty, filling, and delicious—capable of winning over die-hard carnivores (78 West Street, 207-288-4422).

18 EPI SUBS & PIZZA

The best sub sandwiches in Bar Harbor. Inexpensive and filling. Great for take-out/picnic lunches (8 Cottage Street, 207-288-5853).

19 GALYN'S

Coastal cuisine in a relaxed atmosphere. Great for seafood. Open for lunch and dinner (17 Main Street, 207-288-9706).

20 HAVANA

Gourmet, Cuban-inspired cuisine. Upscale, elegant, and delicious. Pricey, but worth it. Open for dinner (318 Main Street, 207-288-2822).

21 JORDANS RESTAURANT

Hearty, diner-style food. Bustling with local charm. Eating at Jordans feels like stepping into a Norman Rockwell painting. Opens at 5am every day, perfect for the sunrise crowd. Breakfast and lunch (80 Cottage Street, 207-288-3586).

22 LOMPOC CAFE

Tasty food with an earthy, Mediterranean/Middle Eastern flair. Part pub, part relaxed outdoor cafe. Huge selection of microbrews (36 Rodick Street, 207-288-9392).

23 MICHELLE'S

Fine dining at one of the most expensive restaurants in Bar Harbor. French cuisine with a New England flair. Gets high marks for blue-blooded elegance (194 Main Street, 207-288-0038).

24 MIGUEL'S

Classy Mexican food. Their outdoor patio is the perfect place to slurp down margaritas on a warm summer evening (51 Rodick Street, 207-288-5117).

25 ROSALIE'S PIZZA

Mouth-watering pizza made fresh from scratch. A cheap way to feed a big family. If you like garlic, Rosalie's Choice pizza (garlic, spinach, mushrooms) is divine (44 Cottage Street, 207-288-5666).

26 RUPUNUNI

Upscale bar and grill. Serves jazzed-up American fare in the heart of Bar Harbor. Their outdoor seating area is great for people watching (119 Main Street, 207-288-2886).

27 TESTA'S

A Bar Harbor classic. Serves reasonably priced seafood with an Italian flair (53 Main Street, 207-288-3327).

28 2 CATS

One of the most popular breakfast spots in Bar Harbor. The ambiance is hip and homey—the food is spectacular. The only downside is the often long wait. Open for breakfast and lunch (130 Cottage Street, 207-288-2808).

BEST OF THE BEST

Best Breakfast: Cafe This Way, 2 Cats
Best Budget Meals: EPI, Rosalie's
Best To Impress: Havana, Michelle's
Best Seafood: Burning Tree

BARS & NIGHTLIFE

If you're looking for nightlife, look no further than Bar Harbor. Literally. It's the only town on the island with any nightlife to speak of. Luckily, there's a wide variety here.

26 CARMEN VERANDAH

The undisputed king of Bar Harbor nightlife. On hot summer nights the dancefloor is packed with sweaty 20-somethings looking to blow off some steam. But despite the predominantly younger crowd, the clientele is filled with all ages. It's not unusual to spot white-haired millionaires or fun-loving matrons soaking in the excitement. DJs or bands perform most nights, and every other Monday Carmen Verandah hosts a drag show where local queens prance and preen for charity.

29 GEDDY'S

Neon lights, TV sports, and cheeky nautical decorations—Geddy's is Bar Harbor's version of Margaritaville. In fact, whenever Jimmy Buffett docks his yacht in Bar Harbor, Geddy's is his watering hole of choice. One of the most fun-loving scenes in town, a place where attitude is thrown overboard and everyone just wants to have a good time.

26 JOE'S SMOKE SHOP

This tiny gem of a bar seats about a dozen, offering a relaxed, chatty atmosphere. Joe's was initially conceived as a cigar lounge, but shortly after it opened Maine banned smoking in bars—literally taking the smoke out of Joe's. But a well-stocked humidor still offers fine cigars for aficionados.

22 LOMPOC

Any bar that serves microbrews on tap and Pabst Blue Ribbon in a can finds a special place in my heart. But even without the PBR, the Lompoc's leafy outdoor patio and playful bocce court would earn it major respect. Bands perform on weekends, adding a folksy, jazzy soundtrack to the mellow, friendly atmosphere. If you've ever swapped Grateful Dead bootlegs or decorated with tapestries, the Lompoc is definitely on your wavelength.

30 THIRSTY WHALE

Stripped bare of pretension, the Whale is where year-round locals go to throw one or ten back. Compared to bars that specifically cater to tourists, the Whale can seem a bit rough and tumble. But that's all part of its charm. Darts and Red Sox—a New England drinker's heaven.

SEAL HARBOR

S EAL HARBOR IS a tiny village with few tourist attractions—and its ultra-wealthy residents would like to keep it that way. Ox Hill, which rises above the eastern shore of Seal Harbor, is home to some of the most expensive homes in New England. But drive along its twisty roads and all you'll see are tiny wooden signs proclaiming the oh-so-elegant names of the mansions lying at the end of the long, long driveways. "Felsmere," "Keewaydin," "Glengariff"—when it comes to Seal Harbor mansion names, the more *Lord of the Rings* the better. Down on Main Street, high-priced shops and boutiques are conspicuously absent from a town that probably boasts a greater net worth than most developing countries. And such tourist-luring establishments are unlikely to arrive anytime soon.

Although Seal Harbor is known (or not known) for its stealth wealth, the town's otherwise low profile was thrust into the limelight with the arrival of Martha Stewart in 1997. After purchasing Skylands, an estate once owned by the Ford family, Martha devoted entire episodes of her TV show to the refined life she enjoyed at her new summer hideaway. Suddenly, domestic divas everywhere knew that Seal Harbor was the *real* place to be on Mount Desert Island. But despite the temporary commotion, the horsey-set residents simply hunkered down and let the excitement pass, and today the tiny village remains as charming and lackluster as ever. In fact, Seal Harbor is probably the most under-appreciated town on the island. Most visitors simply drive by with little more than a passing glimpse of the picture perfect-harbor. But Seal Harbor's tiny town green and jewel-like beach are great places to avoid the crowds and soak in the scenery. So grab a wicker picnic basket filled with fromage and crackers—Seal Harbor awaits.

In 1910 President William Howard Taft visited Seal Harbor on vacation. As he sailed into the harbor a crowd of eager onlookers gathered near the shore. But when Taft disembarked and stepped onto the town dock, his 300-pound frame started to tip it over. As the horrified crowd looked on, a swarm of greeters rushed to his aid, partially submerging the dock under several inches of water. Such marked President Taft's soggy introduction to Mount Desert Island.

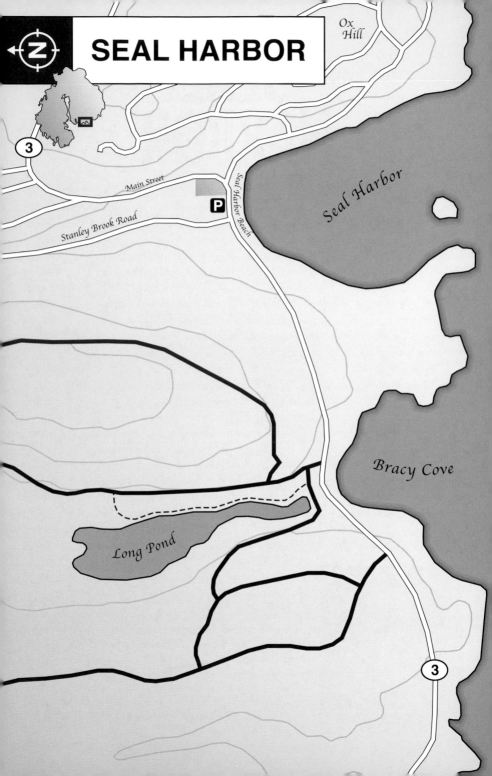

SEAL HARBOR

Ox Hill

3

Seal Harbor

Main Street

P

Seal Harbor Beach

Stanley Brook Road

Bracy Cove

Long Pond

3

SKYLANDS

One of the most spectacular mansions in Seal Harbor is Skylands, built by the Ford family and currently owned by Martha Stewart. When Henry Ford's son Edsel decided he needed a summer home in Maine, he set his sights on Seal Harbor. In 1922 Edsel purchased 80 wooded acres and commissioned architect Duncan Chandler to design a palatial estate. When completed three years later, Skylands boasted a main house, guesthouse, play house, squash court, tennis court, extensive gardens, and a stable. The name Skylands was chosen to reflect the building's stunning views.

Martha's
Bad Behavior

Long before Martha Stewart was targeted by the Feds, her character was assassinated by an even more intimidating group: Maine locals. After purchasing Skylands in 1997, the rumor mill set to work grinding up Martha like gourmet sausages. For the first couple years, barely a week would pass without some new tale of Martha's bad behavior spreading like wildfire across the island. Accounts of Martha storming the kitchens of restaurants where she had reservations, cutting the line at stores, and snatching up the best produce at local farmers markets were swapped with glee. But there was one story that transcended mere gossip and grew into island lore.

As the story goes, one fine summer day Martha burst into a store and demanded to use the phone. "There's a pay phone outside," responded the owner. Martha glared. Again she demanded to use the phone. "I *said* there's a pay phone outside," repeated the irritated owner. At this point Martha lost it. "Don't you know who I *AM?!?*" she howled. Suddenly a soft-spoken gentleman turned to Martha and said, "Ma'am, I'm David Rockefeller. In this town, we all use the pay phone outside. Here's a quarter. Use the phone outside."

As sensationally salacious as the story is, Mr. Rockefeller denies it ever happened. But the speed with which the story spread—and the extent to which it still lingers—speaks volumes about Martha's chilly reception on Mount Desert Island. And dozens of stories of Martha's bad behavior remain...

NORTHEAST HARBOR

I F SEAL HARBOR is a town of stealth wealth, Northeast Harbor is becoming a town of wealth on prominent display—to the consternation of the Old Money families that have summered here for generations. There once was a time when the Rockefellers, Astors, and Fords drove around Northeast Harbor in beat-up automobiles, hobnobbed at run-down private clubs, wore tattered clothes, and otherwise pretended that they were not, in fact, worth millions of dollars. But in the past decade or two, New Money has slowly crept in, bringing bigger yachts, fancier cars, and other forms of conspicuous wealth to prove that they *are*, in fact, worth millions of dollars.

To further compound the problem, in 2003 *W* magazine ran a profile of Northeast Harbor titled "The Wasps Nest." Fear swept over some summer residents that their Old Money hideaway had finally been exposed. The thought of Mount Desert Island ever becoming the next Martha's Vineyard or, worse, *Hamptons*, had many blue bloods coughing up cheap grilled cheese sandwiches at the ultra-exclusive Northeast Harbor Swim Club (where the food served is *soooo* not New Money). But to date, P. Diddy has yet to motor into the harbor and pop open a bottle of Cristal. And despite the unsavory influx of a few billionaires who actually earned their money, Northeast Harbor appears to be hanging on to its relatively low profile just fine. Old Money types still spend their days thumbing through the prestigious "red book"—a tiny, secretive directory listing the names and addresses of the Northeast Harbor/Seal Harbor elite—and private clubs still have decades-long "waiting lists" for New Money interlopers wishing to apply.

But despite the private drives, private clubs, and other private enclaves, Northeast Harbor remains a fabulous place to visit. And some of its top attractions are—hold your breath—free!

Which is not to say you should leave your credit card at home. Main Street is filled with pricey art galleries (not surprisingly, the best on the island) and other high-end shops catering to gourmet tastes. It's a far cry from Fifth Avenue, but if you've got the money, honey, Northeast Harbor's got what you need.

Ironically, Northeast Harbor was born of rather humble circumstances. In the early 1800s it was home to farmers and fishermen. The first summer visitors consisted of artists, clergymen, and intellectuals. When a wealthy New York banker offered to buy a Northeast Harbor farmer's property in the late 1800s, the farmer responded, "We have some very fine people in Northeast Harbor, including a Bishop and three college Presidents. We don't want any Wall Street riffraff!"

My how times have changed...

Asticou Azalea Garden

FREE ATTRACTIONS

1 ASTICOU AZALEA GARDEN

This public garden features over 70 varieties of azaleas, rhododendrons, and laurels that burst with color in the late spring. Even in the summer and fall, the garden is worth a quick visit to soak in the tranquility of the Oriental ornamentation, which includes a Japanese rock garden. The garden is located off Route 198, just north of the intersection with Route 3. Open May to November, sunrise to sunset.

2 THUYA GARDEN *recommended*

Perched on a hill above Northeast Harbor, Thuya Garden is like a secret garden come to life. A half-mile path filled with stone steps climbs up the hill to the garden, offering fantastic views of Northeast Harbor along the way. Thuya Lodge, located next to the garden, offers an extensive botanical library. The garden is open July through September, 7am–7pm. To get to the trailhead, drive past the Asticou Inn on Route 3 and look for the Asticou Terraces parking area on your right. The trail starts across the road at the obvious stone steps.

3 SARGENT DRIVE *recommended*

After the Park Loop Road, Sargent Drive is the prettiest drive on the island. Skirting the eastern shore of Somes Sound, it offers fantastic views of the island's western mountains as they tumble into the sea. Closer to downtown Northeast Harbor, Sargent Drive passes by some of Northeast Harbor's most elegant mansions.

MUSEUMS

4 GREAT HARBOR MARITIME MUSEUM

A small museum devoted to the maritime history of Mount Desert Island. Great for nautical buffs. Open 10am–5pm, Tues–Sat, late June to Labor Day (125 Main Street, 207-276-5262).

5 PETITE PLAISANCE

Petit Plaisance is the former home of French novelist Marguerite Yourcenar, the first woman inducted as an "immortal" into the *Academie Francaise* (a *big* deal in France). When World War II broke out, Yourcenar fled to Northeast Harbor, and once here she decided she could never live anywhere else. Free tours are given by appointment only between June 15–August 31 (South Shore Road, 207-276-3940).

BOAT TRIPS

BEAL & BUNKER

This passenger ferry/mailboat runs trips between Northeast Harbor and the Cranberry Isles (p.257). Departs from the Northeast Harbor Pier. Price: $15 adults, $10 children, $5 bikes (207-244-3575).

SEA PRINCESS CRUISES

Offers sight-seeing trips narrated by a naturalist around Great Harbor, the Cranberry Isles, and Somes Sound. Trips run in the morning, afternoon, and late afternoon. Departs from the Northeast Harbor Pier. Price: $15 adults, $10 children (207-276-5352).

RESTAURANTS

6 FULL BELLI DELI

Fantastic sandwiches. Also offers fresh coffee, tea, and baked goods. Open for breakfast and lunch (5 Sea Street, 207-276-4299).

7 151

One of the best restaurants on the island. Sophisticated comfort food with gourmet flair. Open for dinner (151 Main Street, 207-276-9898).

COLONEL'S DELICATESSEN

A casual restaurant offering burgers, sandwiches, and seafood fare. Open for breakfast, lunch, and dinner (Main Street, 207-276-5147).

Sargent Drive

SOMESVILLE

SOMESVILLE IS SO quaint it hurts. The white clapboard houses, leafy sidewalks, consistently friendly citizens, and impeccably well-tended flower beds are enough to send Martha Stewart scurrying back to Seal Harbor filled with shame. Most buildings here are over 100 years old, landing the town on the National Register of Historic Places. Simply put, Somesville is the kind of town where even thinking about swearing as you walk down the street makes you feel guilty.

Driving down Route 102, traveling at the posted speed limit of 35 mph, you can pass through Somesville in a little under a minute. Blink and you might miss it. But you'll know you're here when you see a gorgeous arched footbridge on the right side of the road—one of the most famous landmarks on the island. Almost all of the town's attractions are located within walking distance of the footbridge, so look for parking as soon as you see it (or use the Island Explorer shuttle, which will stop in Somesville on its way to Southwest Harbor if you ask).

Somesville was the first permanent town on Mount Desert Island. In 1761, 22-year-old Abraham Somes sailed north from Gloucester, Massachusetts and built a log cabin on the shore of this well-protected harbor. The location offered plenty of oak trees (perfect for lumber), several nearby streams (perfect for hydropower), and a saltwater marsh (perfect for hay). The following year, Somes returned with his wife and three daughters. He named the town "Betwixt the Hills," and before long several other families had joined him. By the 1830s Somesville had grown by leaps and bounds. According to one early report it had, "one small store, one blacksmith shop, one shoemaker's shop, one tan-yard, two shipyards, one bark mill, one saw mill, one lath mill, one shingle mill, one grist mill, and one schoolhouse."

Two decades later, the town played a critical role in establishing Mount Desert Island as a major tourist destination. In the summer of 1855, Somesville hosted a large group of early tourists who spent a month at a local tavern. One of the tourists was Frederic Church, a famous artist whose paintings of Mount Desert Island catapulted the island to national fame. But by the time tourists began flooding the island, Somesville was no longer the most important town on Mount Desert Island. Bar Harbor and Southwest Harbor, which lay closer to coastal sailing routes, had become the island's new power centers, leaving Somesville high and dry. Development in Somesville ground to a halt, pickling the town in a colonial time warp that's perfect for modern-day sightseers.

N

102

198

Somes Harbor

Oak Hill Road

3

1

Somes
Pond

2

Pretty Marsh Rd

Beech Hill Rd

102

Beech Hill Cross

MUSEUMS

1 MOUNT DESERT ISLAND HISTORICAL SOCIETY

Located next to the famous footbridge, this small building houses a collection of photographs and antiques relating to the history of Mount Desert Island (207-276-9323, www.mdihistory.org).

SEAL COVE AUTO MUSEUM

Over 100 classic cars are on display at this remote warehouse. The collection includes Rolls Royces, Packards, and Chadwicks. To get there head west on Pretty Marsh Road and look for museum signs. Cost: $5 adults, $2 children. Open 10am–5pm daily, June to September (207-244-9242, www.sealcoveautomuseum.org).

SOUND SCHOOL HOUSE MUSEUM

This former schoolhouse, built in 1892, has been converted into a museum featuring rotating exhibits on Mount Desert Island's cultural history. Open late May to early October, Mon–Sat, 10am–4pm. From the traffic light just north of Somesville, head east on 198 and drive 1.5 miles. Look for a yellow building on the left (207-276-9323, www.mdihistory.org).

ENTERTAINMENT

2 ACADIA REPERTORY THEATER

Performs classic plays and an annual Agatha Christie mystery. Open from late June to late August. Showtime: 8:15pm, Tues–Sun. Children's plays are also offered at 10:30am Saturdays and Sundays in July and August. Tickets: $20 adults, $10 children. Keep your eyes out for a wooden sign on Route 102, just south of the Somesville footbridge (207-244-7260, www.acadiarep.com).

BOOKS

3 PORT IN A STORM BOOKSTORE

One of the best selections of any small bookstore in Maine, including an extensive local section. If you like books, you'll *love* Port In A Storm. The staff here is extremely friendly and knowledgeable (207-244-4114, www.portinastormbookstore.com).

RESTAURANTS

MOTHER'S KITCHEN

Mother's Kitchen isn't actually in Somesville—it's several miles north on Route 102. But their sandwiches are *so* good that they're worth a quick mention (Route 102, tucked away in a small shack next to a hardware store—look for the sign that says "Real Good Food," 207-288-4403).

SOUTHWEST HARBOR

S OUTHWEST HARBOR IS the largest town on the western side of Mount Desert Island. Although it caters to summer visitors, it remains a predominantly "local" town. But when the tourist crush on the eastern side of the island becomes a bit too overwhelming, Southwest Harbor is a great place to get away from it all. Some of the best dining on the island is found here, and there's some fantastic swimming and hiking nearby.

In the mid-1800s, Southwest Harbor was *the* town on Mount Desert Island. It had the busiest harbor and was the center of most commercial activity. But by the late 1800s, when the island became a popular summer resort, tourists avoided Southwest Harbor due to the overwhelming stink of the town's lobster cannery. Before long, cannery-free Bar Harbor had become the new "it" town on Mount Desert Island.

These days the cannery is gone—and Southwest Harbor is definitely on the up and up. Real-estate prices have skyrocketed in recent years as more and more savvy summer home buyers have discovered Southwest Harbor's low-key charm. But despite some mild gentrification, much of Southwest Harbor remains the same. Fishing is still a prominent occupation, and boat building continues to define the town; Hinckley Yachts manufactures ultra-luxe vessels on one side of the harbor, while local artisan Ralph Stanley crafts smaller wooden boats on the other. (In 1999 Stanley was awarded a National Heritage Fellowship for his accomplishments as a master boat builder.) The sense of history and tradition runs deep in Southwest Harbor—with a sprinkling of modern luxury to boot.

Southwest Harbor's Lobster Problem

In the late 1800s, when Southwest Harbor was home to a large lobster cannery, a travel article in *Harper's* magazine lamented, "The objections to landing at Southwest Harbor present themselves before you have taken the first step. Right at the pier there is an extensive lobster house, where the creature is taken out of big tanks, pitched alive into kettles of boiling water, in which he is kept until he is done red, then tumbled out again, torn limb from limb, the meat and marrow plucked from his bones, and crammed into tin cans ... Just as [tourists] are about to be ushered into this new world of romance and delight, to be met upon the threshold by thousands of lobsters, raw, boiled, cooked, and canned, is discouraging, to say the least."

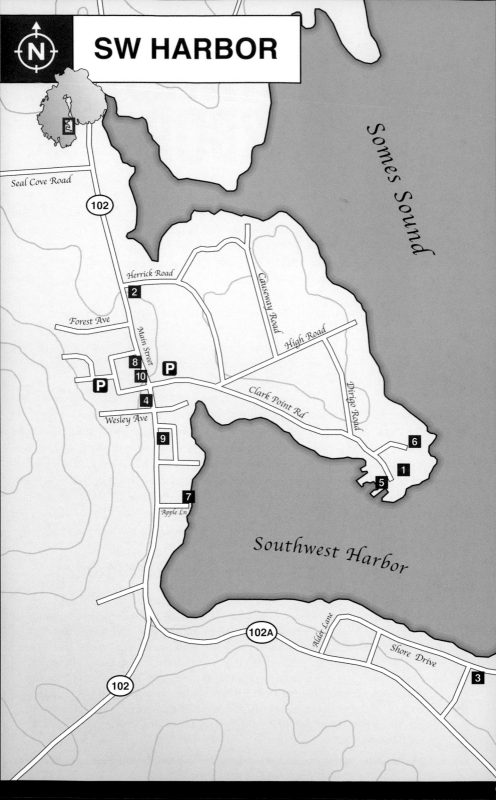

MUSEUMS

1 SOUTHWEST HARBOR OCEANARIUM

This small museum features enclosed tanks of live Maine sealife and a touch tank filled with intertidal creatures—great for kids. This is the sister site of the Bar Harbor Oceanarium. Small admission fee. Open 9am–5pm, Mon–Sat, mid-May to late October (Clark Point Road, 207-244-7330, www.theoceanarium.com).

2 WENDELL GILLEY MUSEUM

Displays over 200 beautiful wooden bird carvings by late Southwest Harbor artisan Wendell Gilley. An excellent spot for avian aficionados. The museum also offers woodcarving demonstrations and workshops. Small admission fee (41 Herrick Road, 207-244-7555, www.wendellgilleymuseum.org).

OTHER ATTRACTIONS

3 HINCKLEY YACHTS

The original "If You Don't Know How Much It Costs, You Can't Afford It" boat builder. Hinckley crafts some of the most prestigious vessels in the world. But even if a new yacht is out of your price range, their company store is still a great place to pick up shirts, hats, and other affordable Hinckley gear (Manset Shore Road, 207-244-7100, www.hinckleyyachts.com).

OUTDOOR ADVENTURES

Acadia Mtn. (p.190) and Beech Mtn. (p.192) are two great hikes nearby. Echo Lake, just north of Southwest Harbor along Route 102, offers great swimming.

4 SOUTHWEST CYCLE

Rents bicycles and offers advice for biking day trips to offshore islands. Open year-round (370 Main Street, 207-244-5856).

RESTAURANTS

5 BEAL'S LOBSTER PIER

There's nothing fancy about Beal's, but this tiny shack serves up some of the freshest, best lobster on the island (Clark Point Road, 207-244-7178).

6 CLAREMONT INN DINING ROOM

Southwest Harbor's most exclusive inn opens its dining room to the public for breakfast and dinner (jacket and tie requested for dinner). Pricey, but offers incredible views of Somes Sound. Their waterfront boathouse is open for cocktails 5:30pm–9pm in July and August (22 Claremont Road, 800-244-5036).

7 DECK HOUSE RESTAURANT/CABARET THEATER

Dinner followed by a cabaret theater filled with singing and dancing. Reservations are recommended during peak season. Open mid-June to mid-September (11 Apple Lane, 207-244-5044, www.thedeckhouse.com).

8 EAT-A-PITA/CAFE 2

Serves healthy pita sandwiches and smoothies by day, delicious upscale meals by night (326 Main Street, 207-244-4344).

9 FIDDLER'S GREEN

Gourmet dining with plenty of international influences—Guiness steamed mussels, sake-infused melon, thai chile relish, etc. (411 Main Street, 207-244-9416).

10 LITTLE NOTCH CAFE

Fresh bakery with tasty focaccia bread sandwiches. Also offers soups, pastas, and desserts (340 Main Street, 207-244-0108).

SEAWEED CAFE

This hidden treasure serves up fantastic Maine seafood, often with Asian influences. Also home to the island's best sushi (146 Seawall Road, Route 102A, 207-244-0572).

BASS HARBOR

BASS HARBOR IS a small fishing village located near the southern tip of Mount Desert Island. It's about as far away from Bar Harbor as you can get—both figuratively and literally. There are few tourist attractions here other than a gorgeous lighthouse, some low-key seafood restaurants, and plenty of quaint coastal charm. If you're visiting Mount Desert Island for the first time, Bass Harbor can be skipped. But if you find yourself intrigued by genuine fishing villages—or disillusioned by tourist crowds—Bass Harbor is worth a visit.

Bass Harbor (the actual harbor) is located in the town of Tremont, which includes the villages of Bass Harbor (on the eastern side of the harbor) and Bernard (on the western side of the harbor). Near the head of the harbor is a beautiful saltwater marsh that's lured people for thousands of years. Indians gathered grass from the marsh and wove it into beautiful baskets. Early settlers used the marsh as a source of hay for their animals. Today the marsh is part of Acadia National Park, luring people for nothing more than its beauty.

For decades Bass Harbor was also the summer hideaway of renowned chef Julia Child, whose family owned a house overlooking the harbor. It was there, long before she became famous, that Julia honed her cooking skills, spending hours experimenting over an old steel stove. In many ways, Bass Harbor is a lot like Julia was: unpretentious, charming, and delightful.

TOP ATTRACTIONS

1 BASS HARBOR LIGHTHOUSE *recommended*

One of the most beautiful lighthouses in Maine, and the only lighthouse on Mount Desert Island. (It's claimed that Bass Harbor Light is the most photographed lighthouse in Maine, but how anyone came to that statistic is beyond me.) Built in 1858 to guard the entrance to Bass Harbor and Blue Hill Bay, the light was fully automated in 1974. The keeper's residence is currently occupied by the Southwest Harbor Coast Guard Commander. A steep staircase to the left of the light descends to a beautiful, rocky vantage point. To get to Bass Harbor Light, head toward the junction of Route 102 and 102A and follow the signs. An Island Explorer stop.

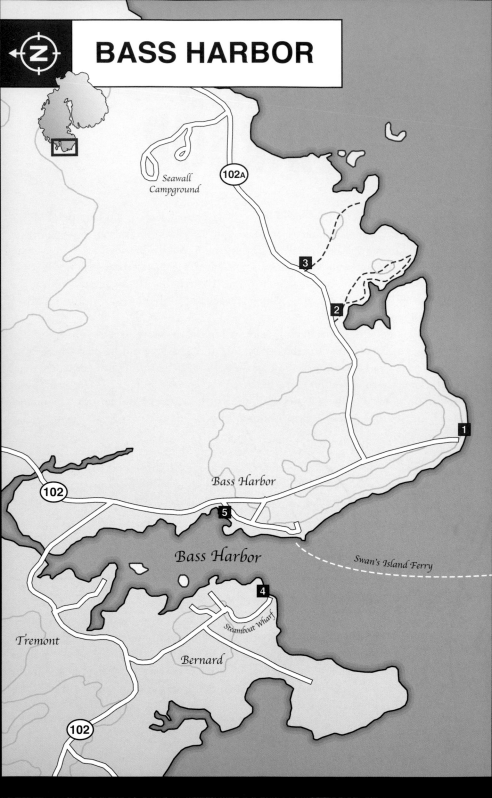

Seawall
Campground

102A

3

2

1

Bass Harbor

102

5

Swan's Island Ferry

Bass Harbor

4

Steamboat Wharf

Tremont

Bernard

102

Bass Harbor Lighthouse

TOP ATTRACTIONS

2 SHIP HARBOR NATURE TRAIL

This 1.5 mile loop skirts Ship Harbor, passing by a saltwater marsh and revealing some of the island's most peaceful scenery. Ship Harbor is named for a Yankee ship that ran aground here while escaping a British gunboat during the Revolutionary War. This is an easy hike with a few rough patches.

3 WONDERLAND

This short, easy stroll leads to a beautiful cobble beach. The trail begins by a small parking area off Route 102A.

RESTAURANTS

4 THURSTON'S LOBSTER POUND

The best place to eat lobster on Mount Desert Island. It's hardly fancy, but the scenery is fantastic and the lobster is divine (Steamboat Wharf Road, 207-244-7600).

5 SEAFOOD KETCH

Moderately priced seafood. Their lobster-seafood casserole recipe was requested by *Gourmet* magazine (McMullin Ave, 207-244-7463).

Bass Harbor

Salt Marsh

CRANBERRY ISLES

T HE CRANBERRY ISLES are five small islands lying just off the southern shore of Mount Desert Island. Although geographically close to the big island, they are in reality a world apart, offering a genuine taste of "real" island life among a small, tight-knit community of Maine lobstermen. In the summer, year-round locals are joined by wealthy summer residents and artists who come to bask in the idyllic scenery. Although tourist attractions are limited, a trip to the Cranberry Isles is worth it simply for the stunning offshore views of Mount Desert Island.

The Cranberry Isles consist of Islesford (also known as Little Cranberry Island), Great Cranberry, Sutton, Baker, and Bear Islands. Islesford offers the most tourists attractions, including a restaurant, a museum, and several shops. Great Cranberry is the largest island, home to a small museum and a quaint gift shop. Baker Island is owned by Acadia National Park, which offers ranger-led tours of the island (check the *Beaver Log* for scheduled trips). The last two islands, Sutton and Bear, are occupied by summer residents, making them essentially off limits to tourists.

In 1755, about 10 years before permanent settlers arrived on the Cranberry Isles, Ebaneezer Sutton purchased Sutton Island from local Indians for two quarts of rum. In the 1970s, booze once again left its mark on the Cranberry Isles when Old Milwaukee filmed a beer commercial here featuring local lobstermen living the good life—surrounded by scantily clad models. (ABC News later used a clip from the commercial as a example of why beer commercials should be banned from television.) Back then, the work-hard, play-hard mentality of some of the young lobstermen led locals to joke that Islesford was a, "quaint drinking community with a lobstering problem." Things have mellowed out considerably since then, but the convivial attitude of the friendly islanders remains.

GETTING TO THE CRANBERRY ISLES

BEAL & BUNKER

This mailboat/passenger ferry runs daily trips from Northeast Harbor to the Cranberry Isles. Price: $15 adults, $10 children, $5 bikes (207-244-3575).

CRANBERRY COVE FERRY

Runs daily trips from Southwest Harbor to the Cranberry Isles from May to mid-September: Price: $15 adults, $10 children (207-244-5881).

The Cranberry Isles

MAINE ISLANDS

In the 1800s, over 300 islands in Maine were populated year-round. Back then, the islands offered unbeatable access to fishing grounds and coastal shipping routes. But as cars, trucks, and motorboats revolutionized commerce in the 1900s, many islanders relocated to the mainland. Today, only 14 islands in Maine continue to support year-round populations.

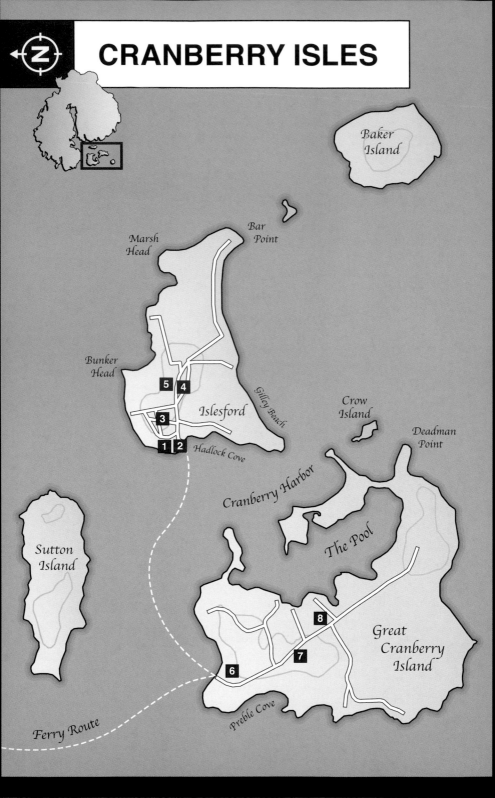

GETTING TO THE CRANBERRY ISLES (continued)

WATER TAXIS

Two water taxis offer private rides to the Cranberry Isles: the MDI Water Taxi (207-244-7312) and the Delight (207-244-5724). Cost: about $45.

ISLESFORD (LITTLE CRANBERRY ISLAND)

1 ISLESFORD HISTORICAL MUSEUM

This small museum, operated by the National Park Service, focuses on local maritime history. Open daily, mid-June through September (207-288-3338).

2 ISLESFORD DOCK RESTAURANT

Fresh seafood and amazing views. Open for lunch (except Sunday) and dinner, late June through Labor Day. Also offers a Sunday brunch. Note: Unless you've got your own boat, you'll have to catch a water taxi back after dinner. (Islesford Town Dock, 207-244-7494).

3 ISLESFORD ARTISTS

This excellent gallery showcases the works of Islesford's vibrant artistic community. Open daily in July and August; open weekdays the rest of the season (Mosswood Road, 207-244-3145, www.islesfordartists.com).

4 THE ISLESFORD MARKET

A small market selling pizza and other snacks. Open Mon–Sat, mid-June to Labor Day (Main Street, 207-244-7667).

5 BRAIDED RUGS INN

The only lodging on Islesford. Rates run about $70 per night, breakfast included (Main Street, 207-244-5943).

GREAT CRANBERRY ISLAND

6 CRANBERRY GENERAL STORE

A small general store selling snacks near the town dock (207-244-5336).

7 HISTORICAL MUSEUM

Showcases an eclectic collection of historic artifacts. Open late June to mid-September or by appointment (Main Road, 207-244-3594).

8 WHALE'S RIB

A small giftshop (Main Road, 207-244-5153).

Hockamock Head Lighthouse

SWAN'S ISLAND

S WAN'S ISLAND IS a gorgeous island lying six miles southwest of Mount Desert Island. Accessible by ferry from Bass Harbor, it features one of the best protected harbors in Maine (famous with boaters) and 7,000 acres of classic coastal scenery. Home to roughly 360 year-round residents, Swan's Island is like an island trapped in time. Other than satellite TV and the Internet, little has changed over the past several decades, and the island's tight-knit fishing community continues to live a life that revolves entirely around the sea. If you're looking for the salt of the earth, it doesn't get much saltier than Swan's Island.

Swan's Island also boasts one of the most colorful histories of any island in Maine. When French explorer Samuel Champlain first set eyes on it in 1604, he named it *Brule Cote*, "Burnt Coast" (presumably because wildfires had recently burned the island). Over the years, *Brule Cote's* pronunciation and spelling was twisted and mangled to "Burnt Coat"—the current name of Swan's Island's famous harbor. Even today, Swan's Island continues to engage in linguistic lawlessness. Since 1986, island residents have made a deliberate attempt to restore the historically accurate apostrophe to Swan's Island—in defiance of nautical charts and the U.S. Postal Service.

Swan's Island's first white settler was Thomas Kench, who fled here after going AWOL during the Revolutionary War. For over a decade Ketch lived here as a hermit. Then one morning he awoke to find settlers arriving by boat. He was horrified to learn that the island had been purchased by his former Revolutionary War commander, Colonel James Swan. Apparently, tensions between the Colonel and his former soldier had eased considerably by then, for Ketch lived on the island an additional 10 years before moving to the mainland.

To populate his new island, Colonel Swan offered 100 acres to any homesteader who promised to stay at least seven years. The first man to accept this offer was David Smith, who arrived here from New Hampshire in 1791. Over the course of his life, Smith fathered 27 children by three wives, earning him the local nickname "King David." (Most Swan's Island residents can still trace their lineage back to King David.) At its peak in the late 1800s, Swan's Island boasted a population of over 700, and its fishermen were consistently ranked first or second in Maine in terms of annual catch. Back then, mackerel was the most profitable catch. But as American tastes shifted, lobstering, which was formerly the domain of old men who could no longer fish, became the island's most popular occupation. During the 1900s, when the gas-powered engine made fishing from the mainland possible, the island lost over half its year-round population. The islanders that remained, opting for an isolated life dictated by the sea and the weather, are perhaps the ultimate embodiment of rugged individualism in America today.

Burnt Coat Harbor and Hockamock Head

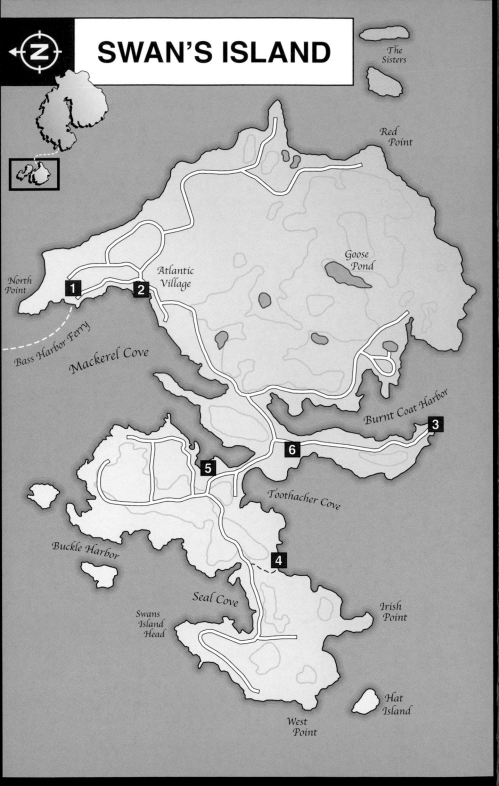

GETTING TO SWAN'S ISLAND

CAPTAIN HENRY LEE

This 17-car ferry makes several daily trips between Bass Harbor and Swan's Island. Call the Maine State Ferry Service for current schedules and reservation information (207-244-3254, www.state.me.us/mdot/opt/ferry/ferry).

Note: The handful of tourist attractions on Swan's Island are fairly spread out. If you visit, it's a good idea to bring your car. Another option is to bring a bike, but you'll burn plenty of calories covering the island's often hilly terrain.

TOP ATTRACTIONS

1 LOBSTER & MARINE MUSEUM

A small museum that displays antique fishing equipment.

2 SEASIDE HALL MUSEUM

Another small museum, this one devoted to local history.

3 HOCKAMOCK HEAD LIGHTHOUSE

This handsome lighthouse, built in 1872, guards the entrance to Burnt Coat Harbor. Hockamock Head is the only spot on the island that retains its original Indian name, which has been translated as both "Evil Spirits" and "Place on the Other Side."

4 FINE SAND BEACH

The jewel of Swan's Island. One of the most beautiful beaches in Maine.

5 ATLANTIC BLANKET COMPANY

This upscale company is run by former Boston lawyers John and Carolyn Grace, who quit their jobs over a decade ago, relocated to Swan's Island, and became full-time weavers. Their exquisite (and expensive) creations are handwoven from local wool. Open Mon–Sat, 2–5pm (888-526-9526, www.atlanticblanket.com).

6 HARBORWATCH MOTEL

The only lodging on Swan's Island. Also offers bike and kayak rentals. Open year-round (800-532-7928, www.swansisland.com).

SWEET CHARIOT MUSIC FESTIVAL

In early August, private boats fill Burnt Coat Harbor to revel in three nights of singing and storytelling. By day, musicians serenade boats in the harbor. At night, performances are held onshore in Oddfellows Hall.

Fine Sand Beach

the remarkable life of
JAMES SWAN

The story of James Swan, the first owner of Swan's Island, is one of the most colorful tales in American History. In 1675, when Swan was just 11 years old, he arrived in America from Scotland. By age 17 the ambitious, self-taught youngster had written a book arguing against the Slave Trade, making him one of America's earliest Abolitionists. Later, he joined the Sons of Liberty, participated in the Boston Tea Party, and fought at Bunker Hill (where he was wounded twice). Following the war, he was elected to the Massachusetts State Legislature. Not long after that he inherited a vast fortune from a wealthy Scotsman who, though not related to Swan, had deeply admired the young man's ambition. Swan used the money to purchase and sell confiscated Tory property, making a second fortune in no time.

Armed with newfound wealth, Swan led an increasingly flamboyant lifestyle. He speculated in risky investments, fought (and won) a duel, and boasted of owning the most luxurious horse-drawn carriage in America. In 1786 Swan purchased Swan's Island and most of the small islands surrounding it. He referred to his property as his "Island Empire" and built a grand mansion on Swan's Island where he entertained guests in lavish style.

But just one year after purchasing Swan's Island, many of Swan's risky investments turned sour. To make up for his losses, he invested in even riskier ventures. When trace amounts of gold were discovered on Swan's Island, Swan spent huge sums of money establishing a full scale mining operation. Three years later, the mining operation had produced enough gold to make "one good sized wedding ring."

Swans debts compounded with astonishing speed, and he was forced to flee to Paris to escape his creditors and try to rebuild his fortune. Using aristocratic connections, Swan landed several lucrative contracts with the French Army, but the contracts fell apart with the onset of the French Revolution.

Swan escaped the guillotine, but he was later arrested by French authorities for an alleged debt of 2 million francs. Although Swan had the money, he insisted that he did not owe it and refused to pay—a noble stance that landed him in prison for the next 22 years. While incarcerated, Swan paid off many of the debts of his fellow inmates, but he refused to even speak with the man who claimed he was owed 2 million francs.

By the time Swan was finally released from French prison, he was 76 years old. His wife and most of his friends had passed away. Having nowhere to go, Swan returned to prison and pleaded to become an inmate again. His offer was refused. Three years later, Swan died alone on a Paris street.

INDEX

Books

Photographs

Travel Information

www.jameskaiser.com